UNDERSTANDING THE
PROPHECIES
OF THE
MILLENNIUM

John Stitt

Edgar C. James

UNDERSTANDING THE
PROPHECIES
OF THE
MILLENNIUM

EDGAR C. JAMES

ISBN: 0-8024-5141-1

1 3 5 7 9 10 8 6 4 2

Printed in the United States of America

To my wife Barbara

my daughters Sharon and Brenda

my son-in-law Kevin

my grandchildren Jessie, Blythe, and Grace

and my many wonderful students

who have given me much help, support, and love

CONTENTS

PREFACE

Living the fast-paced life of the third millennium, we are struck with the advances of the past and the prospects for the future. We clone animals, fly space shuttles, rocket to planets, talk on wireless phones, and constantly use the Internet. Our generation is privileged, as Bill Gates said, to communicate "at the speed of thought" (Bill Gates, *Business @ the Speed of Thought*, Warner Books, 1999).

Our modern world has accomplished much, and yet we see large areas of need. Many children go hungry, uprisings occur throughout the world, government officials become corrupt, families break up and the definition of "family" is revised, school children are shot for no reason. Why can't the many technological advances of our generation solve the moral problems of the world?

Man has tried the social sciences and has failed. He has tried human government but nothing happens. He has tried technology and has given up. We are still faced with murders, rapes, racism, and loose morals.

The fact is that the world has turned its back on its Creator. It has no time for God. The rapid discoveries of science have overshadowed the fact that God is still on His throne and has a plan for this world. He will not be thwarted by the age of man. He will accomplish His will in the nations of the world as well as in our own lives.

I am amazed at the turn of events during these past few years. More and more we see God's Word fulfilled. Peoples and events are turning out just as God predicted millenia ago.

It is important to step back from our hurried world and see God's plan for the future. What will God do with the nations of the world, nations like Euroland, Russia, China, Japan, and the United States? What is happening in our world to show us how soon Christ must return to solve the moral problems of man and to set this world right? Could it be that He will return this year or in the next few years? And if God is moving all things toward the goal of accomplishing His purpose, can He not take care of you and me and the problems we face as we seek to live for Him?

Perhaps you would like to be born in another time and face another set of problems, maybe problems that are a lot less complicated. But that, of course, is not possible. When you stop to think about it, this is our special time, our generation, and we are responsible for it. It is my prayer that all of us will realize the strategic time in which we live and see the significance of God's hand in this world. As a result, I pray that we will be motivated to use our time and talents according to God's plan—while we still have time.

Edgar C. James
Wheaton, Illinois

— 1 —

THE WORLD, THE MILLENNIUM, AND MODERN PROPHECY

On a warm, sun-scorched afternoon, fourteen people sit cross-legged in the middle of a centuries-worn, limestone plaza. Here, on the temple Mount in Jerusalem, they discuss how they will face the end of the world. They and their leader are planning the "big provocation," the event they hope instigates war between Arabs and Jews—a war that culminates in Armageddon, the final conflict.

They have assembled in this city from Denver, Colorado. This well-disciplined cult group believes their inspired leader will die on the streets of Jerusalem. Then, like Christ, he will be raised from the dead three days later. "Prepare to follow me and die," he exhorts his followers, all seeking the promised admission into paradise.

Not only cult groups but also ordinary people plan for the end of the world. In Lisbon, Ohio, an automotive technician and his family sock away a gas-powered generator, dehydrated food, and a waterbed. If the utilities fail, the waterbed will come in handy, for it contains 300 gallons of water. In Harrison, Arkansas, people hold town meetings on economic survival. In rural Montana, underground shelters are ready and stocked with nonperishable bulk foods. The pattern repeats itself across the globe.

Through the centuries, many people have prepared for the world's destruction. William Miller, a nineteenth-century farmer, led one of the largest movements. On October 22, 1844, he and fifty thousand followers fled to the hilltops and waited in vain for his announced appearance of Christ (*Herald of the Midnight Cry: William Miller and the 1844 Movement.* Paul Gordon). These and others have looked for Christ's second coming only to be disappointed.

Now that we're living in a new millennium, we wonder what's going to happen next or if we, too, should plan for the end times. Will life continue as we know it, we ask ourselves, or are we already living on the precipice of the Apocalypse? This is the chaotic period when good and evil do battle before Christ's second coming, the time predicted in the last book of the Bible, the book of Revelation.

All of us are interested in the future, for that is where we will spend the rest of our lives. But how can we have confidence in any viewpoint of the future? Can anybody really know what is going to happen, or is it all a pipe dream? After all, people have tried to predict marriages, politics, and the stock market for years, and nothing seems to work with complete accuracy. How, then, can anybody predict what will happen in this coming millennium?

Some of the predictive sources people try are fortune-tellers, psychics, and prophets, but they haven't worked too well. Desperate people look at the predictions of Nostradamus, extraterrestrial phenomena like UFOs, and the spirit channeling and healing crystals of the New Age. They call the Psychic Hotline or cast their futures upon astrology.

Astrology, the view that the sun, moon, and stars influence human affairs, is enjoying a resurgence. The Sumerians first used it, followed by the Babylonians, the Egyptians, and the Romans. Today major newspapers devote whole columns to it, books and magazines are printed about it, and the Internet contains many astrological sites. Thousands of people buy lottery tickets or plan their lives according to their astrological "signs."

A businesswoman tried astrology. "Our home was very expensive," she confided. "It was secluded on seven wooded acres overlooking the gulf. But when I saw my chart and the way the planet Mars, standing for fires and accidents, and Saturn, standing for restriction and loss, were in exact conjunction with one another, I reached for the phone.

" 'I want to increase my insurance,'" I told my broker. The fire never came, but at least I was protected!"

People also follow their own dreams and visions. "I've had a good life, but I haven't been happy," a woman told me. "My husband is a good man, a leading surgeon in this city," she continued. "But when we were going together, we had many arguments and were about to break up several times.

"During a rather stormy argument, I had a dream," she said. "In my dream I saw an angel at the foot of my bed who said, 'Go ahead and marry him, and I will bless the marriage.' I married him, but life has been anything but peaceful. I wonder if dreams really can be trusted."

Although psychics, planets, and dreams may reflect our own thinking and therefore relieve psychological pressure, they are unreliable guides to the future. They only mirror our own images. They do not provide clear answers.

"In college I took many hours of philosophy," a friend told me, "and I found out that no one can predict the future."

And that's just the point. How can any humanly contrived system give accurate guidance for the future? How can such systems do anything but extend the historically established patterns of human history? They cannot predict change. They cannot predict outside forces. And if they cannot do that on an individual level, how can they do it on a national or world level?

You don't have to be born with a crystal ball to know the future, however. Many who make right decisions are not necessarily fortune-tellers or cult leaders, but they are able to find accurate information and act upon it. And when they have carefully searched, often they have found information not from man, but from God. The most reliable source regarding future events is the Bible.

The God-given Book of Scripture was written hundreds of years ago but is especially relevant to our lives as we live in this millennium. Many use its pages to guide them in personal relationships, marriage, business, and daily ethics. However, there is an area of guidance that is particularly important to us today—the area of prophecy. The Bible has much to say about the future, the interplay of nations, coming wars, natural disasters, and economic up-heavals. It also speaks of a perfect thousand-year period, a millen-nium, that one day will come upon the earth.

We can trust this Book because it is from God. In fact, it even claims to be the Word of God, not man. Thirty-eight hundred times in the Bible there are phrases like "God said," "Thus saith the Lord," and "The word of the Lord came to me." It also says that "all Scrip-ture is God-breathed and is useful for teaching, rebuking, correct-ing and training in righteousness" (2 Timothy 3:16). This means that the source of this material is God Himself, even though He used men to communicate it.

We can also rely on this Book because it gives evidence that God inspired it. For instance, 750 years before the birth of Jesus Christ, an Old Testament prophet predicted He would be born in the village of Bethlehem in Israel (Micah 5:2). How realistic is it to believe that a prophecy of the Messiah's birth would be so literally fulfilled? Certainly a public relations director would have at least picked Rome or Jerusalem instead of Bethlehem for such an impor-tant event. There are many other minutely fulfilled prophecies of His virgin birth, His ministry of miracles and healing, of His death and resurrection (Isaiah 7:14; 61:1–2; 53:6; Psalm 16:10–11).

If the Bible is so accurate in predicting Christ's first coming, we can also rely on it to predict His second coming. It speaks of a king-dom, a thousand-year, millennial kingdom that He will establish here. It may be that the millennium in which we are now living might begin the new millennium of Messiah, and there is strong in-dication of that possibility. However, there are several world events that need to take place before that time begins.

For instance, the Bible predicts the rise of a New Europe in roughly the same geographical location as the Old Roman Empire. It forecasts the influence of a Russia that is able to cause world hav-oc. It predicts the importance of China and where that nation fits in the coming scheme of events. It gives careful details regarding Ar-mageddon, not according to some Hollywood screenwriter's imagi-nation, but according to what actually will happen. And it also predicts a new millennium, a thousand-year period, in which Christ Himself will rule the earth.

This is not some fanciful fairy tale, but a careful unraveling of age-old prophecies that are especially relevant to us as we enter the third millennium. These predictions help us live our lives as we focus on future events. They show us exactly where we fit in, and how we can have purpose for our lives today.

As we unravel some of these significant prophecies, what can we expect them to do for us? First, they will help us understand the *reliability of Scripture*. Much of the Bible, nearly a third, was prophetic at the time it was written. Although there is a great deal yet to happen, many events already have taken place. When we examine history and see how accurate God's prophecies are, we can safely conclude that all of Scripture must be from God. And if the Bible speaks authoritatively in the area of prophecy, it also speaks authoritatively in the other areas of our lives.

We can also expect to see the *power of God*. Many examples illustrate God's power in the past. We see it in the Creation, the crossing of the Red Sea by the children of Israel, and the resurrection of Jesus Christ. But what about solutions to the wrongs and suffering of our world? Family units disintegrate, morality degenerates, and nations bomb to keep peace. Drugs, starvation, and AIDS tear apart global society.

Is there anything that can right the world's wrongs? Is there anything that can solve our problems? The social sciences, human government, and money have all tried and failed. Is there any hope? Do we have to live another century, another millennium to find answers?

Bible prophecy is important, for it shows God's ability to untangle these kinds of knotty questions. There are cases where God has restored families, reduced starvation, and removed the influence of drugs from people. As a result, there is hope that He will relieve completely today's vast suffering, that a better world is coming, that there will be a new kind of millennium.

We can also expect to see some of the *purposes of God*. The future is covered over and none of us in and of ourselves can see what is going to happen. Whenever we make plans, we constantly see them interrupted. When we think we know what is going to take place, the exact opposite happens. But God has pulled back part of the veil, and there are some coming events we can know. He has taken us into His confidence and given all of us a clear message if we will but read and interpret it properly. God has told us in advance exactly what He plans to do. We therefore can perceive many future events, and we can know where we will fit in.

We would live very frustrated lives if all we had were newspapers, news magazines, television reports, and MTV. We would react to each world event, thinking it was haphazard and coincidental. We would wonder if life were worth living, for we would not be able to see any master plan.

But God has clearly disclosed His design. He has told us where this world is headed, what He is doing, and what events need to happen. Without God's knowledge of the future, we would be like ships without rudders. We would not know where to go or how to get there.

As we unravel this important information, we can have *peace for troubled hearts*. Jesus said, "Do not let your hearts be troubled" (John 14:1), and we can have confidence in Him because He is in control.

Anxiety and depression are huge medical problems today. People are frustrated with their leaders and with the failed solutions they offer. But as a child can be at peace in his father's arms even though both are in a storm-tossed ship at sea, we can be at peace in our Father's arms as we live with the problems of our world. It is not circumstances that give peace. Rather, it is where we place our security. When we rest in the center of God's will, we find peace and confidence in the midst of life's storms.

Perhaps the most important expectation we can have is *purity of life*. As we learn what will happen in the future, it affects our daily living. We need to demonstrate the life of Christ in the world in which we live.

Throughout the Bible, the promise of Christ's return is coupled with admonitions on how we should live. For instance, the apostle Peter wrote, "So then, dear friends, since you are looking forward to this, make every effort to be found spotless, blameless and at peace with him" (2 Peter 3:14). The apostle John proclaimed, "Everyone who has this hope in him purifies himself, just as he is pure" (1 John 3:3). The hope of Christ's return should make our present living more holy.

Many are looking to human guides or their own experiences to find instruction for coming events. But since it is God who controls what is going to happen, should we not look to Him? When we do, we will have peace and confidence in Him for both present and future living. Such contentment enables us to demonstrate His life and teaching.

As we live in a new millennium, we face unparalleled pressures and opportunities. Perhaps we wish we were born at some other time of history, but this is God's time for us. And with the responsibility of our generation on our shoulders, how do we make sense out of our world? Where are things headed, what events will happen, and how can we take advantage of the situation in light of God's prophecy revealed to us?

I would like to unravel some of the major prophecies of the future, prophecies of a coming Bible millennium, prophecies that show how close in time that might be. I would also like to share with you how we can take advantage of such crucial information.

— 2 —

WILL THE NEW EUROPE RULE THE WORLD?

On an imposing square in Brussels, Belgium, stands a dignified multistoried building. Across its polished desks and in its busy offices hour after hour, decisions are made which touch the lives of millions in Europe and beyond. Daily, limousines bearing dignitaries from the capitals and commercial centers of the world discharge their passengers for important conferences. Its communications network covers the globe.

This modern hub of activity, the European Union, is the center of a new and rapidly rising world entity. Many, especially outside the continent of Europe, are scarcely aware that it exists, yet there are evidences that already its influence is profoundly felt throughout our world.

Aside from its contemporary role, however, many see in this emerging edifice the shadowy form of a long-awaited structure, the last-days empire described by the prophet Daniel in ancient Babylonia some twenty-five hundred years ago. This is a power which prophecy declares will play a key role in events shortly preceding the second coming of Christ.

The European Union (EU) or Common Market began as the European Economic Community (EEC) on January 1, 1958, when six nations—Belgium, France, Germany, Italy, Luxembourg, and Holland—banded together for economic purposes. Later, Britain, Ireland, Denmark, Greece, Portugal, and Spain were added to make twelve member nations. Currently there are fifteen member nations in the EU, with seven more seeking admission. The express goal of the EEC is the political union of Europe (Anthony Kerr, *The Common Market and How it Works* (New York: Pergamon, 1986), 5–6).

From its inception, people such as Jean Monnet, the spiritual father of the New Europe, have always thought in terms of a ten-nation federation. Some think there could be a realignment of nations with some going out and others coming in. More likely is the prospect that several other nations will join, resulting in a twenty-five - or thirty - nation membership, but with ten principle powers.

All of this is important in that a Bible prophet long ago predicted there would one day come upon the earth a ten-nation federation in the approximate territory of the old Roman Empire. That confederacy would play a strategic part in end-time events. A world empire would turn against Israel and be involved in earth's final world war. Is what we see developing in Europe the fulfillment of the prophet's oracle? Are we witnessing in this millennium the countdown to what the Bible calls "Armageddon"?

The Scriptures predict that in the last days before the return of Christ to earth, there will be four great blocs of nations, or four major confederacies. One of those will be west of Israel, a ten-nation federation. But if what is happening in the European Union today is the formation of this western confederacy, we could well be standing in the starting gate of end-time world events!

What nations will be in that western confederacy? We cannot be sure. However, the rapidly rising structure of the New Europe fits many aspects of the biblical description.

For instance, we know there will be ten major nations. The prophet Daniel spoke of the empires that would rise and fall upon the earth when he explained the wonderful image of Nebuchadnezzar's dream (Daniel 2). That image portrays the whole sweep of Gentile world history.

In Daniel chapter 2, Daniel interprets a dream that King Nebuchadnezzar has in which he sees a statue with a head of gold, chest and arms of silver, abdomen and thighs of bronze, and legs of iron and clay. Daniel explains that the head of gold is Nebuchadnezzar's empire, which will be supplanted in time by different empires represented by the other materials. Many Bible scholars agree that the fourth empire, of iron and clay, is Rome, which was at its zenith soon after the earthly life of Christ. Interest focuses especially on the feet and toes of the image, which we understand to illustrate a reappearance or continuation of that great power to the current time.

Referring to the feet and toes, it is clear that ten kingdoms make up this final Gentile power (Daniel 2:41–42; the number *ten* is also mentioned in Daniel 7:7, 24 and Revelation 17:12, which support the previous passage). Until recent times no such empire had appeared in that part of the world. With the rise of the Common Market, all of that may have changed. Now there is the possibility of ten major nations with many associate nations. (Of course, we can expect changes from time to time in the number of nations and in their geographical location. But in the end, there will be ten major nations that will occupy an area approximately the same as the old Roman Empire. The status of these ten nations may be represented in a governing body similar to the five permanent members of the United Nations Security Council.)

The western confederacy will be powerful. Daniel said that it would "be partly strong" (Daniel 2:42) and "devour the whole earth" (Daniel 7:23). In fact, it is not only to become *a* world power, it is to become *the* world power. "The fourth beast is a fourth kingdom that will appear on earth. It . . . will devour the whole earth, trampling it down and crushing it" (Daniel 7:23).

Up to now that prophecy has remained unfulfilled. No successor to the Roman Empire has ever achieved that kind of power. The empires of Napoleon and Hitler came close, but both proved to be short-term gasps. Through the centuries, continental neighbors have quarreled continually. Again and again, disputes and rivalry have given way to bloody conflict. Twice in the last century nationalism in Europe flamed into global warfare.

Already the total population (370 million EU citizens versus

290 million Americans) and gross domestic product of the EU nations ($9.46 trillion in 1997) exceeds that of the United States ($8.08 trillion in 1997) (*1998 CIA World Factbook*, Washington, D.C., GPO, 1999). The EU standard of living is expected to match America's soon also. Although there are problems, this new confederacy could become the most powerful union economically, politically, and militarily on the face of the earth.

Is it mere coincidence that a long-fragmented continent, separated by different languages, cultures, histories, and traditions, should see the rise of a new federation? To find out what is happening, I visited the European Union's headquarters in Brussels, met with authoritative spokesmen, listened to facts and figures. My conclusion: Despite lingering doubts about integrating economies, standardizing currencies, and delineating national authority, the European Union is on the way to becoming a unified reality.

Already the EU nations represent the world's largest trading bloc. Their gross domestic product is growing. Their population is huge. They have negotiated commercial or association agreements with more than ninety countries. They have special trade and aid relationships with more than fifty former colonies in Africa, the Caribbean, and the Pacific.

That is why, as the EU began, the National Security Council of the United States in a special report stressed its possible global effects.

"In the long run we could be confronted by an 'expanded Europe' comprising a Common Market of at least ten full members, associated memberships for the EFTA [European Free Trade Area], neutrals, and referential trade arrangements with at least the Mediterranean and most of Africa. This bloc will account for about half of world trade, compared with our 15%; it will hold monetary reserves approaching twice our own; and it will even be able to outvote us consistently in the international economic organizations" (Henry Kissinger, *White House Years* (Boston: Little, Brown, 1979), 426). It is interesting how much of this prophecy has been fulfilled.

It is also a political federation. There are only two ways to gain power: one is to take it by force, the other is to be given it. The way this kingdom receives its power is by mutual consent. An interesting passage in the Book of Revelation points this out. Speaking of these nations as horns of power, or kings, it says, "The ten horns you saw are ten kings who have not yet received a kingdom, but who for one hour will receive authority as kings along with the beast. They have one purpose and will *give* their power and authority to the beast" (Revelation 17:12–13, italics added).

When we look at the New Europe, that is exactly what it purports to be—a European federation of states. Each nation maintains its individual identity but has banded with the others for economic growth and protection. All the barriers to trade among member states have been torn down, whereas formerly each nation tried to post heavy tariffs on rival products and goods. A standard tariff is established on products coming into the EU from nonmember countries outside of it.

Though the initial incentives to unity were economic, early leaders wanted much more. "'Political Union,'" said Professor Walter Hallstein, the first president of the Common Market, "is identical in meaning with the 'political unity of Europe,' which the existing Community is designed to bring about and which its founders had in view as their ultimate goal" (Walter Hallstein (*Europe in the Making*, trans. Charles Roetter (New York: Norton, 1973), 293).

The idea of European unity is not new. In 1634 the Duc de Sully of France, in his book *The Grand Design*, proposed a federation of European states. In 1939 Aristide Briand advocated a European federation of states to deal with tariffs, transport, finance, health, social welfare, and technology. Although nothing came of these early proposals, the climate of cooperation to avoid future conflicts after World War II enabled countries to establish the Common Market with these hopes and objectives in view.

The landmark Treaty of Maastricht, signed by the twelve member nations in 1991, brought about substantial unifying regulations while abolishing or minimizing many national codes in each country (Phillipe Barbour, Ed., *European Union Handbook* (Fitzroy Dearborn, 1996), 41). Already there is the free movement of workers between countries. Workers may seek employment anywhere in the Community, though governments retain the right, in some cases, to restrict free movement of labor. Uniform European Community passports have been introduced. The passports bear the title "European Community" above the national designation. There is also the free movement of capital anywhere in the Community. Early leader Jean Monnet was given the title "Honorary Citizen of Europe."

One important goal of European integration was to establish a European parliament voted on by direct elections instead of appointed members, as was done when the Common Market was first set up. This step was taken when a European parliament was directly elected in June 1979. The parliament continues to function, anticipating expanded membership from new nations and expanded powers, as members' national sovereignty is gradually eroded (*Organization of the EU Governmental Body*, http://europa.eu.int, 1999).

Another goal of European integration was to have a common currency that would show political unity and make trade much easier. Such a European Monetary Union was first proposed in 1969, but enactment was slow. The biggest move was taken in January 1999, when eleven European countries (Austria, Belgium, Finland, France, Germany, Ireland, Italy, Luxembourg, the Netherlands, Portugal, and Spain) began using a common currency, the *euro*. Beginning with stock, bond, and bank transactions, it spread to the circulation of coins and notes. With a common currency, many of the impediments of political union will be removed. The euro is scheduled to become the standardized currency of member nations on January 1, 2002.

Not surprisingly, the introduction of the euro and its more centralized monetary management policies are likely to bring about reduced democratic freedoms and civil rights. EU citizens will be forced to relinquish current national democratic involvement in favor of more distant EU monetary (and thus political) leadership and decision making (Andrew Martin and George Ross, "Europe's Monetary Union," (*Current History* April 1999), 171).

The western confederacy also has a potential military arm. Operating through the North Atlantic Treaty Organization (NATO), the principle European countries have been seeking to maintain and enforce peace in the region. In the aftermath of the Cold War, when NATO's energies were directed at containing Soviet expansionist efforts, NATO is now seeking to redefine itself as a regional security agency. The recent war in Kosovo and Serbia has demonstrated NATO's willingness to use force to bring feuding nations in line, even those not belonging to the EU or NATO (Lally Weymouth, "Stopping the Catastrophe", *Newsweek* (26 April 1999), 32).

Although the US still maintains a critical leadership role in the alliance, the Kosovo crisis showed that European members are taking a greater role in determining and carrying out policies. Evidence of this came during the Kosovo crisis in April 1999 when the German government made German troops available for operations in the region, the first time German troops have gone into combat since World War II (Speech by German Defense Minister Manfred Woerner, 17 April 1999, www.nato.int/docu/facts/bpfy-htm).

Speaking at the annual meeting in Washington, D.C., Secretary General Javier Solana said, "Even as NATO is adapting, so is Europe. The European Union has adopted a common currency and a Common Foreign and Security Policy. It is only natural that NATO reflects and helps support this evolution. That's why I foresee an alliance with a stronger European identity...("The Washington Summit: NATO Steps Boldly Into the 21st Century", *NATO Review* (Spring 1999), 6).

Many believe it is from this confederacy that the future Antichrist arises. One day this person will make a covenant with Israel to guarantee that nation protection (Daniel 9:27). But after three and a half years, he will break that covenant and move into the Middle East, even into the land of Israel (Daniel 11:41). It is then that he will lead his confederacy in earth's final world war—the campaign leading to Armageddon. Many in Europe, tired of the long-standing factional disputes and conflicts among neighboring states, seem ready for such a leader who can unify the continent and bring lasting peace and prosperity to Europe.

How close is all of this to the return of Christ? Although we are warned against setting specific dates, Scripture points out a most significant fact: The western confederacy will be in existence when Christ returns to the earth. Daniel wrote, "*In the time of those kings, the God of heaven will set up a kingdom that will never be destroyed*" (Daniel 2:44, italics added). The Lord of heaven will crush that confederacy and set up His own righteous kingdom upon this earth.

It is possible there may be changes in boundaries and nations in that confederacy before the return of Christ. But the fact is that the European federation bears a striking resemblance to the approximate boundaries of the Roman Empire. If what we are witnessing is the formation of the long-awaited revived kingdom, we may ask: "How much longer will it be before Christ returns?"

Today these countries enjoy a rich Christian heritage and ministry to other nations of the world. It was in Europe that important evangelists preached and taught, and it was from Europe that the gospel spread to new lands. But the newness of Christianity has worn off, and many people have grown cold and indifferent to the greatness of God.

Perhaps God is putting it on the minds of some of His people to go back to this one-time center of Christianity and minister to a wonderful new generation. The opportunities for evangelists, preachers, and teachers of the gospel abound, and we should make full use of the wide-open doors. As we examine prophetic passages regarding the future of this part of the world, we find that it soon may be too late.

— 3 —

THE RISE OF MILLENNIAL WORLD LEADERSHIP

In a small unpainted flat above the local town bank in Tampico, Illinois, the son of an itinerant shoe salesman entered the world. "Dutch," as his closest friends called him, grew up loving birds, wildlife, and the sport of swimming so much that he worked as a summer lifeguard at Lowell Park along the Rock River. He went on to Eureka College, a small church-related school in central Illinois, where he majored in economics.

From such humble beginnings, however, no one ever suspected that Ronald Reagan would become one of the world's great modern leaders. And yet he influenced millions of people as an entertainment star, the spokesman for General Electric, the governor of California, and as president of the United States.

Ronald Reagan began affecting crowds when he gave "readings" for his mother's theatrical group in Dixon, Illinois. He went on to acting in high school plays, led his college freshman class, dramatized Chicago Cubs radio baseball games, and starred in several Hollywood movies. He demonstrated his greatest leadership as president, however, when he met with Mikhail Gorbachev, Soviet general secretary, and tried to halt the nuclear arms race.

"I told Gorbachev," President Reagan recalled, "that I thought he and I were in a unique situation at a unique time. . . . 'We can agree to reduce arms—or we can continue the arms race, *which I think you know you can't win'*" (Ronald Reagan, *Ronald Reagan: An American Life* (New York: Simon and Schuster, 1990), 13, 15). It was out of that fireside chat along the shores of Lake Geneva, Switzerland, that the arms race abated, the Cold War ended, and modern world history changed forever.

Our world is always looking for great leaders. Sometimes people do not care whether their leaders are good or bad, as long as they deliver what the people want. Because most people are by nature followers, they instinctively look for someone who can lead them through trials and uncertainties. The mass generally lacks the ability to discern whether the right leadership qualities are present in the leaders they choose. Leaders who are charismatic or who promise much often win the hearts and minds of the people over more practical, sensible alternates.

Leadership is especially important in end-time events, for one day an evil leader will come upon the scene who will have great intelligence, charisma, and support. He will influence world economies and cause financial collapse. He will support world religion and then destroy it so the world will worship him. And he will lead nations and empires to fight against each other in earth's final global battle, "Armageddon."

Who is this person that is so powerful and influential? He is known as the Antichrist, the one who is against Christ, God, and the things of God. Because of this, he will try to lead all the people he can to pursue his cruel plans. World conditions will one day rife for just such a persuasive leader, and people will mistakenly follow him.

Some have identified a current evil world leader as the Antichrist, only to be disappointed when he dies. Although Scripture does not specifically name the Antichrist, it does give important characteristics that will aid his identification. For instance, he is the one who has "eyes like the eyes of a man and a mouth that spoke boastfully" (Daniel 7:8).

When one thinks of a person's eyes, he thinks of great wisdom or great intelligence. This is especially true in our day, for we place great premium on education and the intelligence of our leaders. This was not always so. Less than a hundred years ago it was unusual for a person to go to high school, let alone college. Today we want our leaders to have at least a college education and admire those that have additional degrees, like law or business. The Antichrist will be admired for his insight and wisdom as he offers solutions to current problems. Were he alive today, he might find a ready audience in many parts of the world.

Another mark of this person is his boastful mouth, or pride. From time to time, all of us have prideful hearts, but this person's pride will consume him. He will seek to use people and move them to please himself. He will try to change times and laws so he can have his own way.

We have had many modern examples of government officials trying to use laws for their own benefit. When they are discovered, they are prosecuted, tried, and sometimes imprisoned. Such corruption causes many people to become indifferent toward government and not vote. However, good government results when all of us investigate the backgrounds of candidates and vote only for those we believe have the moral background and right philosophy to hold the privileged office they seek.

The Antichrist will have a prideful behavior and his followers will easily accept him. People will put their faith in him without really examining him. They will think that this is just another leader following the pattern of abuses so many before him have already done.

The Antichrist will be a world leader. Webster defines leadership as the act of "directing, commanding, guiding," like the conductor of an orchestra. Although people have goals they want to accomplish, leaders give them encouragement to attain them. However, sometimes people follow charismatic evil leaders with wrong goals. How else can one explain the suicide missions of Jim Jones and his followers in Jonestown, Guyana or the thirty-nine men in the People's Gate Cult in the million-dollar mansion north of San Diego?

The Antichrist will be a political leader. He will head the revived Roman Empire, the new confederacy of nations that arises out of the old Roman Empire, now known as the Common Market. He will use his unchecked political power to exalt himself and subdue his enemies.

The world has periodically sought to have a supergovernment. Nations cannot solve problems themselves, so large groups have banded together to solve their problems. In 1814, near the end of the Napoleonic Wars, Austria, Russia, Prussia, Britain, and France met at the Congress of Vienna and formed the Holy Alliance. It quickly broke down because conflicting interests and territorial ambitions ruined it.

The world made another attempt at the end of the First World War when they established the League of Nations. However, internal bickering and global indifference emptied it of any real power. Finally, the victorious Allied Powers created the United Nations in 1945 at the end of the Second World War. This forum proved successful in resolving several conflicts, including the Persian Gulf War against Saddam Hussein. A strong United Nations has the potential of becoming a one-world government.

The Antichrist will arise from the revived Roman Empire, the land of NATO and the European Union, and seize political authority. That rise to power will come not as a result of warfare, but rather individual states will give their authority to the Beast (Revelation 17:13). Although there could be numerous changes before this occurs, it is interesting how the current political order is postured to support such a transition.

The Antichrist will be a religious leader. Throughout world history many wars were fought in the name of religion. The Crusades, perhaps the most famous of religiously based conflicts, tried to expel the Moslems from the Holy Land during the Middle Ages. Northern Ireland, Iran and Iraq, the former Yugoslavia, and the whole of the Middle East have engaged in recent religious conflicts.

In contrast to such divisions, the ecumenical movement seeks to unite various denominations and world religions. Eventually, the Antichrist will acquire this ecumenical group and destroy it. He will do this so he can become the world's major religious person. He will establish himself in the temple of God, call himself God, and seek the world's worship (2 Thessalonians 2:4). He wants to destroy all religion so he can forge his own. This is why he is called "Antichrist."

He also will be a military leader. He will lead a large coalition of nations against the military powers of the world in a final world battle called "Armageddon" (Revelation 16:16). He will honor a "god of fortresses" and wage war with saints, the people of God (Daniel 11:38; 7:21). He is against the plans, purposes, and program of God.

The Antichrist will not act alone. Another leader, a False Prophet, will help him accomplish his purpose (Revelation 13:11–18). This individual will arise out of the earth or land, probably a reference to the land of Israel, pointing to his Jewish heritage.

The major purpose of the False Prophet is to get the world to fall down and worship the Antichrist. To do this, the False Prophet will perform spectacular miracles such as causing fire to come down from heaven for all to see. This is what the prophet Elijah did, and some will think this person is also a prophet from God. By imitating the power of God, the False Prophet will easily be accepted by the people, and he will get them to fall down and worship the Beast.

He will make a gigantic image of the Antichrist. This image will be animated so it looks lifelike and real. By being able to make the image speak, the False Prophet will have a profound effect upon the world and be able to compel the people to do as he directs.

The world will receive the special mark of the Beast or Antichrist. This mark will be visible and placed on the right hand or forehead of the people. Its operation may be similar to the way credit cards or grocery items are scanned at a check-out line, via a subcutaneous implant under the skin. This requirement will have great economic significance, for no one will be able to buy or sell items without it.

The number of the Beast is 666. Probably the best interpretation is that this number represents man, for man was created on the sixth day of creation. People are used to such numbers today with social security numbers, area codes, and zip codes, so no one will be surprised at one more. What the Antichrist and False Prophet will do represents what man will do at the zenith of his civilization. Man left to himself and his own devices tries to glorify himself. He wants to worship himself and his achievements, rather than recognizing any help God may give.

Although it may appear that the Antichrist and False Prophet do all of these things themselves, they will have a lot of help. They will have a very sympathetic people who are ready for such things, but they need leadership, an evil leadership to do these terrible deeds. Then, too, Satan also will energize the Antichrist and the False Prophet. He will influence them and make them carry out his plans and purposes. He will get them to do what he wants them to do. With all of these influences, the people will turn against the Lord of heaven.

Who is Satan about whom we hear so much? Although he has tried to deceive the world regarding his own existence, the Scriptures in many places attest to his reality. For instance, even Jesus talked about him (Matthew 4:1–11; 16:23; 25:41; Luke 4), and he is mentioned from Genesis to Revelation.

Satan originally was created by God as an angel and was an anointed cherub, a being that protected God's holiness (Ezekiel 28:13–14). He was privileged to be in the very presence of God until he sinned against the Lord of Hosts. Now his motive is to defy God and to do all he can to tear down what God is building up.

Jesus described Satan in very uncomplimentary terms. He said he was a murderer from the beginning and also a liar (John 8:44). Those are not nice characteristics, but they are true. Satan cannot change, and he always acts according to his nature.

Satan's design is to counterfeit the plans, purposes, and program of God. When Satan sinned against God, five times he said in his heart, "I will" (Isaiah 14:13–14). He was trying to substitute his own will for the will of God. He was attempting to usurp the power and authority of the Lord Himself, for he wanted to be *like* God, to be a counterfeit of Him (Isaiah 14:14).

Being a counterfeit is seen in his appeal to Eve as he tempted her to sin. He enticed her by saying that if she sinned, she would be "like God" (Genesis 3:5), a sign that she would be part of Satan's counterfeit system.

This is his same appeal to people today. He is not an angel that some think is dressed in black or long, red winter underwear with a pitchfork in his hand. Not at all. Rather, he is seen as an angel of light (2 Corinthians 11:14). He wants to be as acceptable as possible, for he has his own plans and programs, which are anti-God.

During a coming Tribulation period he will try to set up his own world government and use the Antichrist and False Prophet to accomplish his goals. He will try to get the world to worship his people, the ones he will place in world leadership.

What is the eventual doom of Satan? Today he is allowed, through the long-suffering of God, to mislead the world. However, when the Lord comes to set up His kingdom here on the earth, He will bind Satan and throw him into the Abyss (Revelation 20:3). After the thousand-year reign of Christ upon the earth (the Millennium), Satan will be released from his prison to deceive the nations (Revelation 20:7). Then he will be taken and thrown into the lake of burning sulfur (Revelation 20:10).

If all of this happens to Satan when Christ returns to the earth, what will happen to the Antichrist and False Prophet? When Christ comes to set up His kingdom, He is going to deal with them. He is going to take both of them and throw them alive into "the fiery lake of burning sulfur" (Revelation 19:20). God will tolerate them for a time so that the world will see what happens when there are no restraints and man is left to himself. But judgment is coming, as it always is, and God will throw them both into eternal damnation.

These are the leaders of the world during a yet future time. They will move the nations of the world to war against each other. Our world today is being so staged that it is now waiting for the rise of the Antichrist and False Prophet.

Is it possible that these future evil leaders already could be alive? Many have tried to identify them in history, but these have not turned out to be *the* Antichrist or *the* False Prophet. However, if this end-time period is right around the corner, it is possible that these evil leaders may already be alive. I don't believe we know exactly who they are, but it is true that the world is getting ready for them. As a result, we also need to be prepared.

All of us are leaders in our own right, even though we may not think of ourselves in that way. However, we have leadership roles in our families, our work environment, our churches, and our communities. All of us have centers of influence, and many look up to us whether or not we realize it. As a result, we need to be positive role models in all we say and do. People want to follow someone, and if it is us, we should give them a good example.

One day the world will follow bad examples and be led astray. But that day is not here yet. We need to exert a positive influence wherever we can, while we still have time.

– 4 –

WILL RUSSIA SCARE
THE WORLD WITH
GLOBAL DISASTER?

A long the weather-worn, red-brick street, the tired crowd waits for hours. The line is not as long as it used to be, but a dispirited remnant of masses continues to file past the embalmed lifelike body in its granite tomb. They come on the anniversary of his death to pay their respects to the memory of Vladimir Lenin, the Russian Communist leader who led the 1917 revolution.

These mourners remember the proud Soviet state and the iron-fisted regime that once ruled their world. Back during the "nanny" government, they had jobs, education, health care, a place to live, and a cradle-to-grave security that is now but a distant memory.

Since the end of the Cold War, Russia has changed its whole social structure. Some insiders, who obtained state-run oil, energy, and mineral businesses, profited handsomely. Many, however, lost their jobs, health, and wealth. Adult Russian men witnessed their life expectancy drop from sixty-four to fifty-nine in just eight years. They saw their life's savings evaporate through runaway inflation, an inflation that sometimes approached 3,000 percent. They observed their government leaders argue, revolt, and the government change hands. But in spite of all the problems, however, the Russian nation continues to survive.

Now the question is: Will the new Russia ever regain the glory of its former days? Without question, events have stifled Russian efforts to be a leading player in world affairs. There have been diplomatic pushes here and there, but world opinion, European democratization, and their own economic problems have held the Russians in check. However, the Russians are not remaining idle in asserting their presence. As if to remind the West that their strategic reach and military potential is not dormant, in June 1999 Moscow sent four nuclear-capable bombers on a duel-flight mission around Iceland and a long the Norwegian coastline (Richard J. Newman, "The Russians Are Coming", *US News and World Report* (12 July 1999), 39).

The IMF (International Monetary Fund) gave the Russian government billions of dollars to get her house in order. As a result, the Russian leadership has tried to move the country toward a more free market policy. But gigantic deficits and inefficiencies continue and many wish for the good old days of the Communist state. The ultranationalist Vadimir Zhirinovsky concluded, "The conditions in Russia are now as ripe for a revolution as they were in October 1917" (*U.S. News and World Report* (8 February 1999), 36).

Recent world events remind us of the shakiness of this age and the constant turmoil of governments. Continued economic and political strife in Russia, as well as any movement back toward strains of communism would be a major problem ("Russia's Puppet Master", *Time* (23 August 1999), 36–37). Russia's large inventory of nuclear, chemical, and biological weapons gives it a devastating war-making potential that few other nations possess. President Yeltsin recently intimated that Russia would lead an armed struggle against the NATO coalition operating against Serbia over the Kosovo crisis if the West did not address Russian concerns ("A New Cold War?", *World Press Review* (July 1999), 8).

Some Bible scholars believe this is significant, for Russia still possesses a latent capability to wage war against its neighbors or move into the Middle East. While Russia no longer fears Israel in the way it once did under the Soviet regime, it is deeply concerned about the disruptive spread of Islamic fundamentalism into Russia's southern border regions. For that reason, and its desire to restore economic ties to former Arab client states like Iraq and Syria, Russia is profoundly interested in the Middle East.

Given the historic volatility of Middle Eastern politics and Russia's need to placate or eliminate Islamic fervor along its southern borders, an alliance of Arab states with Russia against Israel again is possible ("A New Cold War?", *Time* (23 August 1999), 38). Such a conflict might trigger the Battle of Armageddon in fulfillment of Bible prophecy. Are we close to such a possible scenario today? We can only wait and see.

Before Christ returns to the earth to set up His kingdom and rule the nations, four confederacies will surround the land of Palestine. One of those will be a great northern confederacy that will come down against the land of Israel and there be destroyed by God. It is possible that nations already may be arranging themselves to become that northern confederacy without ever knowing it.

Twenty-five centuries ago a Bible prophet spoke of a day when a great northern confederacy would march into the Middle East. He told how that would happen in Israel's "future years," the time when Israel would exist as a nation and under world protection so that she could dwell in "unwalled villages." Although the peace process in Israel is a continuing concern, the United States and Western European nations have consistently supported the inviolability of the Israeli nation against foreign threats. With such conditions presently existing in Israel as the prophet described, it could be that we should soon expect the coming together of a northern confederacy. Perhaps what we are witnessing with Russia and her foreign policy endeavors is the assembling of a northern bloc of nations that will eventually result in a Middle East move.

What are the countries of the northern confederacy? Russia is a major one. In the vision of the prophet Ezekiel, God told him to set his face against "Gog of the land of Magog, the prince of Rosh" (Ezekiel 38:2, NASB). Although those names seem strange to us, Hebrew scholars such as Gesenius, Keil, and Lowth point out that the name *Rosh* (sometimes translated "chief") stands for the people of the modern nation of Russia. Bishop Lowth wrote, "Rosh, taken as a proper name, in Ezekiel, signifies the inhabitants of Scythia, from whom the modern Russians derive their name" (John Cumming, *The Destiny of Nations* (London: Hurst & Blackett, 1864), n.p.). The message then describes Gog, the symbolic leader of the land of Magog, that is, the prince of Rosh, or nation of Russia.

Confirming evidence is that this confederacy will come from the "far north" (Ezekiel 38:6, 15; 39:2). A careful look at a globe shows that the city of Moscow is almost on the same longitude as the city of Jerusalem. Since the known world of the first century A.D. did not include much beyond the coastal settlements along the northern shore of the Black Sea, a logical conclusion to the reference "far north" suggests the present-day lands of Ukraine or Russia.

What other nations will be aligning themselves with Russia? It may be possible that Russia will regain some of its former mystique and unite with countries that once formed the Soviet Union, although Scripture does not indicate that. The prophet does say that other countries will join with Russia. One of those countries is Libya, an African state far removed from Russia geographically but united with her in foreign policy ("Put," Ezekiel 38:5). Another nation is Ethiopia, also an African state, precariously balanced between chaos and stability, which has maintained good relations with the Russians in the past and which has persecuted Christian converts and missionaries ("Cush," Ezekiel 38:5). A third country is Persia, the modern country of Iran (Ezekiel 38:5). Iran has recently moved closer into the Russian camp by signing new arms deals to upgrade the Iranian military. Russia has long been suspected of providing nuclear technology assistance to the Iranians following the collapse of the Soviet Union. The Iranians may even possess some former Soviet nuclear weapons as a result of clandestine government sales or the Russian black market. The current alignment of nations is almost the same as Ezekiel predicted.

Why will the northern confederacy come against Israel? It is because of greed—to take the wealth of Israel, the "spoil" from the land (Ezekiel 38:12–13, NASB). Throughout history great powers have known that the land of Israel was essential as they sought to expand their empires. The region is the nerve center of communication among three continents, a land bridge between Asia, Africa, and Europe. Alexander the Great made conquering Israel the goal of his Grecian empire. The caesars of Rome made Israel part of their empire. Is it any wonder that Russia and her allies should also want this "golden jewel"?

Russia also needs the area for its economy to flourish. Russian access to sea trade has historically been restricted. Murmansk on the Arctic Ocean and St. Petersburg on the Baltic Sea are frozen over for parts of the year. Russia's limited seaports on the Black Sea are further restricted by the need to have her ships pass through the choke point of the Turkish-owned Dardanelles, a route easily closed in the event of hostilities. Russia needs access to the Mediterranean and Indian Ocean seaports year-round for trade to improve her flagging economy.

Ezekiel says that Russia's coming against Israel is because Russia wants to plunder gold and silver, livestock and goods. Throughout the centuries great wealth has gathered in the Middle East, wealth such as agriculture in Egypt, dates in Saudi Arabia, and cedars in Lebanon. Why would a nation with the vast natural resources of Russia want such spoil?

That was the question until the discovery of oil. Suddenly, the Middle East took on an entirely new significance. Today the riches of the world are flowing into the Middle East because of the value and necessity of that precious commodity. In a day when the need for energy is so great and energy is so unevenly distributed, the nations that control oil control the world.

Until recently, one of the largest oil-producing nations in the world was the Soviet Union. But the breakup of the Soviet Union placed much of Russia's oil production in the newly independent southern states of Kazakhstan, Georgia, Azerbaijan, Turkmenistan, and Uzbekistan. Russia's own oil is running out. New reserves are not being discovered, and the wells presently being drilled lie in western Siberia, which, because of weather and hazards of terrain, are difficult and expensive to drill.

If Russia's oil is running out, where is she going to get more? The obvious answer is the Middle East. Russia directly borders Iran, and an alliance with the Iranians would grant them access to the wealth of the Persian Gulf oil fields. Russia might also threaten Kuwait and Saudi Arabia directly, or support the claims both Iran and Iraq have shown in these two oil-rich countries. From here, the Russians might threaten Israel.

Israel? Why would a world power be interested in a country smaller than the state of New Jersey? There are many reasons. One is that Israel may eventually have oil.

Although only small amounts of petroleum have been discovered in the present land, some experts believe there may be oil in the marine shelf off Israel's Mediterranean shore. It is also possible that Israel's boundaries may change and encompass some oil fields. One day, during the Millennium, the tribe of Asher will "bathe his feet in oil" (Deuteronomy 33:24).

Another reason is because of the Dead Sea. This body of water is one of the richest chemical beds in the world. It contains immense quantities of potash, bromine, magnesium, and other treasures. Potash is a nourishing fertilizer, essential for a nation such as Russia, which, at this time, needs to import much grain. Bromine is important in pharmaceuticals and gasoline, and Russia could use a good deal of that. Magnesium is used in aluminum alloys, important in aircraft construction. It is also used in the making of explosives.

But the Dead Sea offers something else. Israeli scientists have discovered in the water and salt flats the halophilic alga *dunaliella*, which can be converted into petroleum. It is possible that huge "oil farms" may develop in areas south of the Dead Sea where the water could be channeled into saltwater ponds for the growing of *dunaliella*.

The Dead Sea also may produce huge amounts of electricity. In recent years, the water has been dropping due to the diversion of the Jordan's headwaters for farming. Experts envision a channel and tunnel arrangement that would pour the Mediterranean water into the Dead Sea (Harvey Arden, "The Living Dead Sea," *National Geographic* (February 1978), 230). That could become a major source of hydroelectric power, attractive to other nations.

Russia may also want Israel because of her strategic location. Ezekiel says that Israel is the "center of the land," or literally, "the navel of the earth" (Ezekiel 38:12). The control of Israel would provide Russia with important military bases and allow it to dominate the eastern Mediterranean Sea. It would further provide the land bridge between the Middle East and Africa.

There is another reason for Russia's interest in Israel. It is because of Israel's relationship to a great western confederacy. During that future time, Israel will be under the protection of a Western bloc of nations, nations that will be controlled by the Antichrist. A covenant will be made with Israel by this world-domineering confederacy, which will give religious sanctions to Israel for a short time (Daniel 9:27). Could it be that Russia would try to threaten such a great superpower by attacking its strategic protectorate, Israel?

Whatever the possibility of Russia's ambition and greed, few recognized the economic wealth of the Middle East and Israel until recently. Few, that is, except Ezekiel!

What will happen when Russia moves against Israel? When the northern confederacy comes down against Israel in the latter days before the return of Christ to the earth, a strange thing will happen. Instead of Israel fighting and defending herself against Russia, God will utterly destroy that northern confederacy on the mountains of Palestine. God will shower upon Russia "torrents of rain, hailstones and burning sulfur" (Ezekiel 38:22). There will be a shaking in the land so great that even the mountains will be overturned, the cliffs will crumble, and walls will fall to the ground (Ezekiel 38:20). Civil war will break out, for "every man's sword will be against his brother" (Ezekiel 38:21).

Although there may be limited nuclear or chemical and biological wars in the future, this judgment will come directly from God. The Lord Himself will destroy Russia because of her greed and selfishness and because she came against His chosen people. Although He is a God of love, He is also a God of holiness, justice, and righteousness. God must judge all who come against Him.

To see the devastation that such disasters bring, such as earthquakes, volcanoes, and fire, as Ezekiel describes, I flew to the city of Pompeii, Italy. There I witnessed the utter desolation, the complete annihilation of a people that once inhabited that great city. "Why," I asked myself, "did all this come about?" History's answer is clear. It was because of the sin, immorality, and pornography of the Roman Empire. Just as God destroyed the cities of Sodom and Gomorrah and the city of Pompeii, He will destroy a group of nations that come against Him. How much better to know Him today as Savior than to stand before Him one day as Judge!

God will destroy this confederacy because of its selfishness and greed. But He also wants to magnify His name. It is so "they will know that I am the Lord" (Ezekiel 38:23). God's purpose then as now is to glorify Himself. It is to make Himself known throughout the world. And what God is going to do through the nations of the earth, He wants to do through us today. Even though Christ's return may be very close, we should make every minute count for God.

Recently, God has given Christians a window of opportunity to invade Russia and former Soviet countries with the gospel. Many have responded to this call. They have established Christian schools and orphanages and started Bible studies. The ministry has not been easy, however, and governments have clamped down on some areas of service.

However, we must continue to pray and minister while there is opportunity to convey the message to these wonderful people.

— 5 —

CHINA, JAPAN, AND INDIA IN WORLD CONFLICT

In a stately, marble-encrusted building on a majestic, centrally-located square, the specially appointed delegates assemble. Amidst the red carpets and flowers, they hear the yearly economic and political reports. They also make strategic government decisions that affect 1.2 billion people. What they say and do is immediately communicated throughout the most populous country in the world.

These three thousand heavily guarded Chinese people are the National People's Congress, which has ruled this republic for more than fifty years. Once a closed society, this nation now welcomes tourism, business, and trade. It is rapidly moving towards being an important world power in the new millennium. Economic growth increases year after year in spite of protests and problems.

Throughout history, China has worried many. The sheer size of the nation threatens world stability. Even the French general Napoleon Bonaparte said of China, "There lies a sleeping giant! Let him sleep, for when he wakes he will move the world."

China is beginning to dramatically influence world affairs. Her balance of trade with the United States almost exceeds that of Japan. Her military capability is growing. The lessons of wars in Korea, Vietnam, Iran, Iraq, and the Balkans have made her reexamine herself militarily. Already she has the world's largest military (3.1 million troops) and an increasingly sophisticated nuclear arsenal (Frank Gibney Jr., "Birth of a Superpower," *Time* (7 June 1999), 42). Through a sympathetic company she even controls the east and west ports of the Panama Canal. China has an estimated 3,000 "front companies" in the U.S. currently, many of whom seek to acquire sensitive and secret military technology (Tim Healy, "Stormy Passage," *AsiaWeek Magazine* (11 June 1999), 13). She continues to make many advances as she seeks to attain superpower status.

The need for an enhanced military capability occurred when China's industrial base exploded, and she opened her doors to Western peoples. As one Western expert observed, "People's war is good when the society is predominantly agricultural. As the society becomes industrialized, people's war means the sacrifice of the cities, and that means the sacrifice of the nation's security. As the nation develops an industrial base, it has to develop strength along the border to protect the industries" (*Newsweek* (21 January 1980), 51).

All of this is especially significant, for many believe several large Asian nations figure prominently in end-time world events. These countries are the ones that will march with great armies into the Middle East as world history climaxes. As we witness the expansion of China's influence, we also may be witnessing the formation of a biblical eastern confederacy.

Some believe China is mentioned in Scripture as "Sinim" or "Aswan" (Isaiah 49:12), one of the places from which Jews are gathered to inhabit their land. However, the major reference to China and other Asian nations who will march against Israel is the passage that calls them the "kings from the East" (Revelation 16:12).

You and I are living through a time when the nations of Asia are becoming more independent and sleeping China is stirring from her state of slumber. As she awakens, eastern nations are coming together. Is it possible that we are witnessing the formation of "the kings from the East," an eastern confederacy that will have a devastating effect upon the nations of the earth?

During the end times, there will be four major groups of nations surrounding Israel. Two of those, the northern and western confederacies, we already examined. The one we want to examine now, the eastern confederacy, is of special significance. It is the one that, when it invades the Middle East, will culminate in the world's greatest battle as God destroys His enemies at Armageddon.

Who are the kings of the east? Although exact nations are not mentioned, we are told they are nations from the east (literally, "from the rising of the sun"). They also are beyond the Euphrates River (Revelation 16:12). Since the Euphrates River runs across Syria and Iraq and marks the eastern boundary of nations surrounding Israel, this must be a group of Asian nations.

Certainly China fits such a description. Its sheer size, 1.2 billion people, makes it a major power in Asia as well as the rest of the world. With its current awakening, it stands ready to play an active role in eastern and world politics.

The history of China is long and involved with many bright periods. But Mao Tse-tung's Cultural Revolution exhausted it. Now the Chinese hope is to become a world economic and military power. From the opening of China in the early 1970s to normalization of diplomatic relations with the West, China seeks to fulfill its New Long March with a Four Modernizations program. This is an attempt to improve simultaneously agriculture, industry, science, and defense.

As the nation opened to others, the *Peking People's Daily* wrote, "We are setting out to conquer on our New Long March the mountains, seas, plains, oil fields, and mines of our motherland. We want to scale the heights of science and technology. We want to develop normal trade relations with other countries of the world" (*Time* (1 January 1979), 13). Much of this program has been accomplished.

The Chinese proceeded with ambitious vision and vigorously pursued their goals. They completed a seven-year, $13.5 billion trade and cooperation agreement with France. This included two 900-megawatt nuclear power plants, which France built at nearly $1 billion each. They shopped in Britain, Denmark, Sweden, and the United States. They received help in mining, fast-food techniques, and communications. Inter-Continental Hotels built a chain of 1,000-room hotels, complete with swimming pools and saunas. Hyatt International constructed hotels with a total capacity of 10,000 rooms. United, Northwest, and other airlines have scurried for any available landing rights to bring in the tourist trade on a major scale. Much of this expansion is paid for with oil exports, oil that accounted for as much as 19 percent of China's foreign-exchange earnings.

To accommodate their new Western partnerships, many Chinese took crash courses in foreign languages. Millions of copies of Radio Peking's English course were sold in the capital, and some schools taught it. Thousands of Chinese students study overseas. All of this is highly revolutionary for a nation that just a few years ago was decades behind the rest of the world.

The Chinese have invigorated their military by copying the modern weaponry of countries such as Sweden, France, England, and the United States, seeking to offset the obsolescent Soviet models that still comprise the bulk of their inventory (Frank Gibney Jr., "Birth of a Superpower", *Time* (7 June 1999), 42). The government received nuclear secrets from some of these countries, most notably, the United States. The recent disclosures about Chinese complicity in obtaining United States nuclear secrets through contacts in the Department of Energy may enable the Chinese to produce a neutron bomb, a more advanced nuclear bomb, designed to kill personnel while destroying the least amount of property (Sam Cohen, "Check Your Facts: Cox Report Bombs", *Insight on the News* (9 August 1999), 13).

The previous warnings of a Western diplomat increase in gravity and relevance in today's volatile world. "I wonder if an economically and militarily powerful China would be an unmitigated blessing for American interests. Would a China strong enough to threaten Russia in nuclear terms not constitute a threat to us all?" (*Time* (1 January 1979), 19). China also seems intent on absorbing Taiwan, as its recent saber-rattling demonstrations in and around the Straits of Taiwan suggest (Johanna McGeary, "Playing With Fire", *Time* (26 July 1999), 62).

As we observe the Bible phrase "kings from the East," we notice that the word *kings* is plural. This must mean that more than one nation is involved in this confederacy. Could it be that a second nation is Japan?

When we look at Japan, we see that its economic advances are legion. All of us know of its steel production, semiconductor development, television sets, computers, telecommunication equipment, and automobiles. It is a major economic powerhouse. And all of this for a country that imports most of its raw materials and close to 100 percent of its oil.

Under its constitution, Japan cannot maintain armed forces for purposes of aggression. It maintains a national Japanese Self Defense Force and has ships, aircraft, and armored vehicles. Most of its weapons, however, come from the United States.

Because the United States is involved in many world conflicts, some in Japan echo the sentiments of former Prime Minister Masayoshi Ohira. He said, "The U.S. has become one of the powers and not a superpower any more. The days are gone when we were able to rely on America's (nuclear) deterrent" (*Business Week* (19 May 1989), 67). As a result, some in Japan are calling for a defense buildup. Others suggest reestablishing the military draft and increasing military expenditures. Still others urge a review of the country's ban on arms exports. Others want an independent Japan that is not dependent militarily on the United States. To assert its own presence internationally, Japan is now making a concerted effort to establish its own sphere of influence in Africa and the Middle East (Peter J. Schraeder, "Japan's Quest for Influence in Africa", *Current History* (May 1999), 232).

In the midst of these moves for military independence, Japan signed peace and friendship treaties as well as trade agreements with China. Japan exports steel and other goods to China in exchange for Chinese oil. It is possible we may be seeing an eastern confederacy forming in that part of the world.

A third nation that may be part of this confederacy is India. Many believe India is a backward and poverty-stricken nation. However, a careful study shows that this republic possesses great economic and military strength. For instance, India has the tenth largest economy in the world ("India", 1998 *CIA World Factbook*, Washington, D.C., GPO, 1999, 155). It is self-reliant in the manufacture of plants and equipment in major industrial sectors. It has a large pool of scientific and technical manpower. Many countries, including those in the Middle East, rely on India's engineering industry.

All of this greatly enhances India's military capabilities. It produces small arms, ammunition, tanks, aircraft, rockets, and warships. It has the third largest army in the world and an air force that has undergone a billion-dollar modernization program ("India", *1998 CIA World Factbook*, Washington, D.C., 157). Perhaps the most impressive development is India's nuclear research program. That nation detonated its first nuclear explosion in May 1974; improvements in the electronics and missile industries allowed it to acquire advanced nuclear capability by the mid-1980s (Pratep Bhanu Mehta, "India: The Nuclear Politics of Self-Esteem", *Current History* (December 1998), 403). Mutual tests of nuclear weapons by rivals India and Pakistan threaten to bring about a new nuclear arms race (Nayan Chandra, "Waking the Devil", *Far Eastern Economic Review* (11 June 1998)). The United States and other countries played roles in India's nuclear assistance.

Although these nations have military capabilities and may use them to protect their borders, how would they ever threaten the entire world? Are their resources and capabilities sufficient enough?

The world is an ever-changing place and sometimes small nations have their day in the sun. However, these countries are not small and they are moving onto the world stage. For instance, China has the largest number of people on earth and the largest army. In a day when nations rely on their military technology and have reduced personnel manning levels, the Chinese army is maintaining its personnel strength while simultaneously trying to upgrade the technical sophistication of its hardware. Then, too, it is important to observe that the eastern confederacy has its greatest impact on the world right before Christ returns to the earth, some seven years after the Tribulation begins. A great deal of military development can occur in seven years. When we look at the picture from this perspective, there is no question that the stage is set.

Why will these nations come together in a major world confederacy? One reason is economic necessity. Competition with the advanced Western markets will stifle the internal development of Asian markets, notably China and India, unless these markets assert a degree of independence from Western investors. Already there are signed peace and friendship pacts between some of the countries. Also, these nations have similar religious systems. Atheism, Buddhism, and Hinduism are common threads that run through them.

There is also a common concern of Russia. Although these nations sometimes agree with Russia when it serves their interests, China's fear of the Soviets was the major reason she opened her doors to the rest of the world. Russian political instability may result in a more belligerent position with the Asian countries, particularly if they threaten Russia's economic position.

Asian countries eyeing fresh resources to tap into may view the vast mineral resources of Siberia with great fascination. Before the Second World War, Japanese militarists referred to Russia as "the Northern Resource Area," a possible source of materials to fuel the Japanese war machine. Russia's apprehension over Chinese and possibly Japanese designs on Siberia has fostered a requirement to devote sizeable military forces along the Sino-Russian border, including a strong nuclear capability.

If we look carefully at a globe, we notice these three countries—Japan, China, and India—are in a straight line headed right toward the Middle East. These nations, along with others, could form a great eastern confederacy that one day moves against Israel.

Some may ask, "Why do we not see a political union of nations in Asia as we do with the New Europe?" The fact is we do not see it; nor do we necessarily expect it. Scripture points out that the western confederacy will be a federation of states, completely united together (Daniel 2:42; 7:24; Revelation 17:13). On the other hand, the eastern confederacy is made up of independent nations. They are "kings."

Their independence may be the reason they do not appear in end-time events until right before the return of Christ to the earth. It is during the Tribulation that the Antichrist will move into the Holy Land and set himself up as the world ruler. He will then go down to Egypt to take treasures of gold and silver. The kings of the east will allow the Antichrist to do so either because they are aligned with him or because of their own independence and internal problems. But finally, at the end of the Tribulation, they will amass a huge army. They then will invade the Middle East, make war with the Antichrist, and be destroyed when Christ Himself returns (Daniel 11:44; Revelation 9:16; 16:12; 19:11–21).

From what direction will these eastern nations enter the Middle East? They will come from the east across the Euphrates River. The river is somehow dried up supernaturally, which will enable them to cross it (Revelation 16:12).

The Euphrates River is 1700 miles in length and is the largest river of western Asia. It rises in eastern Turkey and flows across Syria and Iraq to the Persian Gulf. It is one of four rivers in the Garden of Eden (Genesis 2:10–14) and is part of the land boundary promised to Israel (Genesis 15:18).

The Asian armies move across the Euphrates because that area forms a natural land bridge from Asia to the Middle East. They also could not come in ships, for the Bab el Mandeb Straits at the mouth of the Red Sea are too small for the many ships required. Then, too, most of Iraq's oil is produced around the Euphrates River. By capturing those oil fields, the Asian armies would ensure themselves sufficient fuel to wage war against the Antichrist.

How large an army will these nations have? There is a Bible passage that gives the exact number in this army—200 million (Revelation 9:16). Although that is hard to believe, it is possible that these nations could quickly assemble that many troops. For instance, in addition to having the world's largest standing army, China has the People's Militia, whose members receive military training in their spare time. This military force is claimed to number 200 million, of which 75 million are women (*Encyclopaedia Britannica*, 15th ed., 4:294). When you think about it, that is not surprising when nearly 40 percent of the Chinese people—500 million of them—are under eighteen years of age.

When the Asian army meets the Antichrist and his army, the greatest war this world will ever see will break out. The nations of the earth will use all of their plans and weapons to try to destroy each other. It is then that Christ Himself will come from heaven and put all His enemies under His feet. He, the King of all kings, will rule the nations with a rod of iron. In contrast to the war of nations, He will establish peace and righteousness on the earth.

As we see the formation of an eastern confederacy, we need to ask ourselves some important questions. Are we making full use of our opportunities for God while we can? And, are we involved in ministering to the wonderful peoples of Asia while we have time? Soon it will be too late!

– 6 –

EARTH'S FINAL CONFLICT

Buried in the midst of a secret, well-guarded military complex, top uniformed leaders analyze, discuss, and plot around a long oval table. They watch as enlisted personnel physically move armament symbols across a large world map that occupies an entire wall. Their eyes scan laptop computers for the latest satellite information, and their ears listen to phone systems connected by push buttons to the world's major political and military centers. This is the war-planning room of a major military power.

As soon as decisions are made and authorization received, they order, through their encrypted phones, missile launches, air strikes, and troop movements. Casualties, civilian suffering, and building demolition results, but this group takes no time to worry. This is war, and in war everybody suffers.

Meanwhile, eight thousand miles away and in sharp contrast to conventional war planning is a quanza-hut desert factory housing three dedicated biochemists. Here, in giant fermenting tanks, bio-agents grow that produce chemical and biological weapons. The most deadly of these agents are the easily made *botulinum* toxin and anthrax.

Anthrax is so potent that, according to TV reporter Diane Sawyer, a five-gallon container sprayed over a city like Manhattan means that in "48 to 72 hours, you're looking at 500,000 people dead" (*Time* (2 March 1998), 57).

Modern wars are fought in many different ways and with many different weapons. Not only can nations use missiles, tanks, and bombers, but they can computer trigger smart bombs, and nuclear bombs. Less sophisticated nations can use chemical and biological weapons that are cheap and easily produced. When countries think war is inevitable, they do not hesitate using all available means to defeat their enemy.

The world is rapidly marching toward its final conflict. Nations try to negotiate disagreements, but sometimes conflict is necessary. Moreover, a few people, with the right chemical and biological mixtures, can start a world catastrophe. But whether by bombs or biological agent, whenever a major war breaks out, we ask, "Is this Armageddon?" Armageddon is the end-time battle when the nations of the earth fight against God and each other in the Middle East. It is the war to end all wars, for a river of blood four and a half feet deep will flow for two hundred miles. Nations will use all the weapons at their disposal since they feel their existence is threatened. There will be winners and losers, but it will be a bloodbath such as this world has never seen.

Many believe that life runs in cycles, and war is just one phase of a much larger life cycle. There are wars and there always will be wars. In fact, Jesus warned that war would constantly occur. He said, "You will hear of wars and rumors of wars" and that "such things must happen, but the end is still to come" (Matthew 24:6).

But Jesus also said there would come a time of "*great distress, unequaled from the beginning of the world until now—and never to be equaled again*" (Matthew 24:21, italics added). The significant fact is that a world-devastating war is part of that unprecedented time period. This war will break out in the Middle East and will usher in the return of Christ. This is why many are looking for such a war at the beginning of this millennium. With growing conflicts in the world and the continual Arab-Israeli discord, some feel such a war could happen very soon.

Sometimes this final world cataclysm is called "the war of Armageddon." Although the place of Armageddon is involved, the Scriptures call this campaign "the battle on the great day of God Almighty" (Revelation 16:14). In other words, the final battle occurs at Armageddon, but there are other conflicts that lead up to that event. Other wars, like World War II, the war in Vietnam, the Gulf War, and the Balkan Conflict, were all made up of many specific battles.

This encounter is on "the great day of God Almighty." Even though planes bomb, soldiers fight, and terrible devastation results, it is a war allowed by God. Nations come to the end of themselves in this conflict, and then God brings it to an end. All mankind fight against heaven and the forces of God, but the Lord and His armies are victorious. As Augustine observed, it is the City of God versus the City of Man, with the City of God the winner.

Where will this war take place? Many Middle East nations think their land will be involved and have tried to protect it with sophisticated weaponry. This is true in Israel, Kuwait, Saudi Arabia, Egypt, Syria, Jordan, and Iraq. The Scriptures, however, predict that the center of the conflict will be Israel. For instance, one of the major battlefields will be Armageddon, for it is there that the nations will gather (Revelation 16:16). *Armageddon* is the Hebrew name for the Hill of Megiddo, a specific place located in the north-central part of Palestine, halfway between the Mediterranean Sea and the Sea of Galilee.

Historically, Megiddo was an important military garrison. It is strategically located and overlooks the valley of Megiddo. This valley empties into the valley of Jezreel, which is the largest valley in the nation. An underground springwater system is there and is necessary for any troops stationed there. As generals tried to take over Israel, and there were many, they knew that if they controlled Megiddo, they would control the whole northern half of the country.

To see the size of Megiddo and to get a feel for its location, I flew to this region. I went through the museum there and relived the history of previous battles. I climbed the hill and looked out over those huge valleys that run farther than the human eye can see. I then thought of the French General Napoleon's remark when he stood at that same place. He said, "This would make the most natural place for the nations of the world to gather for a final war."

There are other battlefields, however, for this bloodshed. One is the Valley of Jehoshaphat. This valley is located in central Palestine between the city of Jerusalem and the Jordan River. This is called the "West Bank" area. God says, "I will gather all nations and bring them down to the Valley of Jehoshaphat. There I will enter into judgment against them" (Joel 3:2). The West Bank problems, like the Jewish settlements, autonomy questions, and the Palestinian State, could be a prelude to a coming war.

Another place for conflict is the land of Edom. This is sometimes called "Idumea" and is located in the southern section of Palestine. The Lord says, "My sword has drunk its fill in the heavens; see, it descends in judgment on Edom, the people I have totally destroyed" (Isaiah 34:5).

Some believe that during future persecution in Israel, some of the people will flee to Edom to escape God's judgment. This is because Scripture predicts that people will hide "in caves and among the rocks of the mountains" (Revelation 6:15). A logical place for them to go is Edom, for it contains many rocks and the capital city of Petra, whose name means "Rock." This was a city that literally was hewn out of rocks and boulders. It contains temples, houses, and amphitheaters, all made out of rocks. However, even though these people try to leave Israel and hide in rocks, they will find bloodshed wherever they go.

The major place of contention, according to Scripture, will be the city of Jerusalem. This city, whose name means "city of peace," has been the object of many wars, and was destroyed several times. It again will be the center of slaughter in this end-time war. God says, "I will gather all the nations to Jerusalem to fight against it; the city will be captured, the houses ransacked, and the women raped. Half of the city will go into exile" (Zechariah 14:2). The problems of Jerusalem's future status may initiate that eventual struggle.

Years ago, former Egyptian President Anwar Sadat began the modern peace movement and went to Jerusalem. There he addressed the Israeli parliament. "The first thing we want," he said, "is the city of Jerusalem!"

Since that time, Arabs and Jews negotiated the Sinai, the West Bank, the Gaza Strip, and a Palestinian State. The problem of Jerusalem, however, continues to fester and could become a time bomb, ready to explode.

The United Nations General Assembly voted for Israel to withdraw from the West Bank, Gaza, and East Jerusalem. Israel, on the other hand, affirmed that the united city of Jerusalem was the country's capital. Of making East and West Jerusalem one, Jerusalem's former Mayor Teddy Kollek said, "Whom did it help? I see what confusion it has created, even among our friends" (*Time* (11 August 1980), 30). The Oslo Peace Accord set the question of Jerusalem aside for a later date. Negotiations on Jerusalem's status continue and temporary solutions have been tried. The underlying attitudes of dissent continue to grow and fester.

The Bible describes the conflict's bloodshed as a harvest of God's wrath, rather than a harvest of souls. The picture is of a huge reaping, the harvest of the whole earth. An angel thrusts his sickle into the earth and gathers the clusters of people from the vine. Then he throws them "into the great winepress of God's wrath" (Revelation 14:19). What a terrible picture of God's necessary judgment because of man's devastating sin.

The description from Scripture continues with a river of blood. This river will flow as high as the horses' bridles, a depth of four and a half to five feet. It will run for a distance of two hundred miles (Revelation 14:20), which is the length of the land of Palestine. With this imagery, God confirms that the entire area of Israel will be covered with the blood of nations, from the northern region (the Valley of Megiddo) to the central (the Valley of Jehoshaphat and Jerusalem), to the southern (the land of Edom).

What countries will fight in this final world war? During end-time events there are four major groups, or blocs, of nations that will surround Israel and come against her. These confederacies are located in the north, west, east, and south of Israel. As we look at the world today, we can see that those blocs of nations may be forming already.

The northern confederacy is Russia and her allies (Ezekiel 38–39). Those nations will come from "the far north" (Ezekiel 38:6) of Israel as a "cloud to cover the land" (Ezekiel 38:9). Russia's continued diplomatic influence in the Middle East, in the Balkans, and elsewhere could be a prelude of what Ezekiel predicted.

The western confederacy is a ten-nation federation located in the approximate area of the old Roman Empire. Carefully described in Daniel 2, it is the last part of the great image in Nebuchadnezzar's dream. This is an image that depicts the entire sweep of Gentile world history.

The New Europe or Common Market may fit the description that the prophet Daniel gave. Many details are precisely as given, while others are potentially working out. As with any new venture, it takes time to assemble all of the right ingredients. However, this confederacy, along with many associate nations, could prepare for the end-time events Scripture predicts.

The eastern confederacy is east of Israel and east of the Euphrates River. It is called "the kings from the East" (Revelation 16:12). China, Japan, and India, with other nations, may make up this confederacy. The overtures those nations are making now could result in the alliance that Scripture refers to.

There is also a southern confederacy. This is where the Arab nations may fit. Instead of this being a multination confederacy, however, this bloc will be just one nation. Typically, there is little unity among Arab countries. Historically, they have spent more time fighting each other than in finding avenues for cooperation. When there is an overriding purpose, though, they can quickly unite. Most of the time, however, they are seen as separate entities. According to prophecy, God has an important purpose for the Arab nations.

The southern confederacy will be most likely be Egypt, for it is called "the king of the South" (Daniel 11). Although Arab states may periodically support this country, the word *king* is singular and shows that Egypt will act alone.

Egypt is a country with limited resources and a vast population. It is a nation of 60 million people, most of whom live in extreme poverty. The government uses 50 percent of its revenue to subsidize basic commodities. The nation is dependent on the handouts of other nations, such as the United States, just to keep going.

Although Egypt is not a leader economically, it is a powerful leader politically. It is the one that began the peace process with Israel many years ago. It is the one that originally obtained land through negotiation. And it is the one that could easily upset the whole easing of tensions in the Middle East.

The way this final war will begin is given in a most illuminating passage. God tells us exactly what will happen. Through the prophet He says that at the "time of the end," Egypt, the "king of the South," will come against Israel (Daniel 11:40). Egypt's pushing against Israel will be an agitation that will initiate the conflict. This will then cause the northern confederacy to come down against Israel to protect its influence.

The underlying reason that Egypt or any Arab nation will confront Israel will be because of the Arab's continued hatred of the Jew. Speaking of the Arab nation Edom, the Lord says it has an "ancient hostility," or a "perpetual hatred" (KJV), of Israel (Ezekiel 35:5). The psalmist confirmed that hatred. The Arab nations have said, "Come. . . let us destroy them as a nation, that the name of Israel be remembered no more " (Psalm 83:4). Also, "with one mind they plot together" (Psalm 83:5).

When Egypt challenges Israel, this will give Russia the excuse to come against that nation. It is then that God will destroy the northern armies on the mountains of Palestine (Ezekiel 38–39).

Up until that time, a balance of world power among the nations will remain. However, when the northern armies are destroyed, the balance of world power suddenly will be no more. This will enable the western confederacy, the revived Roman Empire led by the Antichrist, to move into the "Beautiful Land" (Daniel 11:41). That bloc of nations will then take the treasures of the land, including the "riches of Egypt" (Daniel 11:43). That is also the time when the Antichrist will put himself in the rebuilt temple and call himself God (2 Thessalonians 2:3–4).

The climax of this final conflict will be when the western confederacy, threatened by the kings of the East, will come out of Egypt back to the Holy Land to fight the eastern confederacy (Daniel 11:44). Instead of fighting each other, however, their hatred will turn against the Lord from heaven. It is then that Jesus Christ will return and slay His enemies (Revelation 19:21). The City of God will win, as Augustine said, and Jesus Christ will be victorious!

The hope of the world is not in the nations of the earth or in this world. Rather, the hope of this universe is in the Savior from heaven, who one day is coming to bring in an age of righteousness and rule the nations with a rod of iron. As Nebuchadnezzar learned, "In the time of those kings, the God of heaven will set up a kingdom that will never be destroyed, nor will it be left to another people" (Daniel 2:44).

Two major obstacles to Christian service are peace and prosperity, however. This is because good times rub off on Christians, and sometimes this lulls them to sleep. A close study of church history shows that the church especially grew and developed when it struggled under persecution and when it used opportunities God gave it during times of war.

This does not mean that Christians can serve God only during times of conflict. However, as national battles happen, opportunities for service develop and countries open with evident need for the gospel message. It is important for Christians to be observant of the timing of God, and quickly move in with their message of the hope only God can give. The time of Armageddon is not yet, but the fact that it is coming should keep all of us constantly motivated in our service for God.

— 7 —

MORE TROUBLE
IS COMING

On a calm, bright spring day, eighteen hundred students attended their regular high school classes in a wealthy southern suburb of Denver, Colorado. In the middle of the afternoon, two fellow classmates stormed into the school carrying a semiautomatic pistol, a carbine, and two sawed-off shotguns. They hooted, hollered, shot up the place, and eventually killed twelve students, a popular coach, and finally themselves.

What happened on that terrible April 20 made a nation and world ask, "How could such a tragedy ever occur?" This was the worst of a series of school murders and it happened in one of the best communities. Littleton, Colorado, was the kind of place people sought to escape the crime, drugs, and killings of many urban areas. Students here played sports, acted in plays, participated in honors programs, and joined Bible clubs. If anyplace in the world seemed safe from such disaster, this was it.

The questions regarding cause and responsibility mushroomed quickly. Was the issue easy access to guns by youths, and should government increase their regulation? Were ignorant and irresponsible parents at fault, and should they bear some responsibility? Were the shootings inspired by the violence portrayed regularly in Hollywood movies, video games, and media entertainment, and should these be curtailed or censored? Was the school at fault for not identifying the troubled youths and counseling them earlier? Was it a nation as a whole and should all of us feel a greater sense of responsibility for society's problems?

It could be a combination of all of these causes or some other cause. We feel frustrated at government's and society's failure to solve the problems of drugs, violence, and school killings. We would like to do more to help.

Jesus warned, however, that as the age draws to a close and prepares for His return, crime and wickedness will increase. He said, "Because of the increase of wickedness, the love of most will grow cold" (Matthew 24:12). All of us should help to minimize the vast problems that plague our world. But we also need to realize that the increase of such lawlessness may indicate the closeness of Christ's return.

These problems, along with others, will increase as the age progresses. They will ultimately indicate a time of special trouble on this earth, a time of tribulation. Jesus cautioned about this. He said, "For then there will be great distress, unequaled from the beginning of the world until now—and never to be equaled again" (Matthew 24:21).

Throughout the course of history, frequent lawlessness, earthquakes, famines, and floods have occurred. Wars have devastated regions. Millions have died in plagues. People have murdered since the time of Cain. But Jesus predicted unprecedented trouble that would come upon the earth. It would be different from anything that occurred previously.

Jesus told His disciples they could expect trouble and tribulation in the world (John 16:33). Because the people hated Christ, they would hate those who followed Him. Those who pursued the faith of the disciples would also face such hardships. They would endure the problems and pressures of being servants for God in an ungodly place.

But in Matthew 24–25 Jesus was talking about *unprecedented* trouble that would come upon the earth. Although we may suffer for God today, we are not yet in the time period called "the tribulation" or time of "unequaled great distress." The events of our day, like the disaster at Littleton, as well as the increase of earthquakes and natural disasters, are foreshadowing what is yet to happen.

The physical and spiritual phenomena during the tribulation will be so terrible that God Himself will have to stop it. Jesus said, "If those days had not been cut short, no one would survive" (Matthew 24:22). In other words, if God does not cut short this period of time, the entire world will perish. Jesus, however, is going to interrupt it. He is going to bring it to a close by returning to the earth to set up His kingdom. He will do this so He can rescue those saved during that time.

Old Testament prophets described the Tribulation. They call it "a time of distress" (Daniel 12:1), "a time of trouble for Jacob" (Jeremiah 30:7), and a "day of distress and anguish" (Zephaniah 1:15). Jesus also spoke of that period. He pictured its events to His disciples right before His death.

The disciples showed Jesus the buildings of their brand-new, rebuilt temple. Herod the Great began its reconstruction in 20 B.C., and it would be finished in A.D. 64. It was an exquisite place.

Now, before the Jewish house of worship was completed, the disciples gave Jesus a tour. As they did, Jesus made an unusual statement. He said, "I tell you the truth, not one stone here will be left on another; every one will be thrown down" (Matthew 24:2).

The disciples were dumbfounded. They could not imagine why anyone would destroy a sanctuary so elaborate and beautiful, and so many years in construction. So they came to Jesus privately when He was on the Mount of Olives and asked Him what He meant.

The three questions the disciples asked had ready answers. First, they wondered exactly "when will this happen?" (Matthew 24:3). They were asking when people would destroy the temple. The answer Jesus gave is recorded in Luke 21:20–24. It was when "you see Jerusalem being surrounded by armies" (v. 20).

In A.D. 70, Titus and his Roman armies surrounded the city of Jerusalem for six months while Rome sent them orders to attack. Some people, in literal response to those words from Christ, took the opportunity to flee the city. When the Roman armies ransacked and leveled the city, they destroyed all the people who remained. The city was so devastated that not one stone stood upon the other. The words of Jesus proved true.

The disciples' second question was "what will be the sign of your coming?" (Matthew 24:3). Jesus answered this inquiry in Matthew 24:29–31.

One day many things will happen in the sky. The sun will darken, the moon will stop giving light, and stars will fall (Matthew 24:29). Then the sign of the Son of Man will appear (Matthew 24:30). This is the glory of Christ as He returns. It is then that Jesus will come to the earth to set up His kingdom. He will come "with power and great glory" (Matthew 24:30). His coming to set up His kingdom will be after the Tribulation. There is another time when He is coming, a time when He does not return to the earth, but comes to meet His people in the air and take them back to heaven with Him. This is called "the Rapture," or the snatching away of the church. Many believe that coming of Christ will precede the Tribulation.

The third question the disciples asked was what would be the signs "of the end of the age" (Matthew 24:3). They wanted to know some of the events that would happen before Jesus came to set up His kingdom on the earth. It is this question that Jesus answered first and is recorded in Matthew 24:4–28.

The "end of the age" is that period of time right before the second coming of Christ. It is the time of tribulation when great judgment will be poured out upon the earth. After those devastating events, Jesus will return to put down His enemies and rule the nations with a firm hand. Many of the events we see happening today may foreshadow these events. The act that begins this time period is when the Antichrist signs a special covenant with the nation Israel (Daniel 9:27).

Jesus enumerated many episodes that will take place during the Tribulation. He said, "For many will come in my name, claiming, 'I am the Christ,' and will deceive many" (Matthew 24:5). Although several have claimed to be messiahs down through history, the Antichrist is the one who counterfeits the miracles of God and usurps the worship of God during the Tribulation.

More wars and rumors of wars will occur. The great military

campaign of the Antichrist will culminate in Armageddon, the final battle on earth. Although nations have bombed and soldiers have fought for years, the Tribulation will be a time of unprecedented bloodshed.

What else will happen? There will be famines and earthquakes (Matthew 24:7). These are described in the book of Revelation. Whole cities will crumble (Revelation 6:12; 16:18–19). The famines and earthquakes we see happening today may foreshadow these events as well.

These marks of trouble are just the beginning of that time period (Matthew 24:8). The last half of the period, known as the "great tribulation"(KJV) or time of "unequaled great distress" (Matthew 24:21), will have even more intense events.

There will be severe anti-Semitism (Matthew 24:9), and many will fall away from the truth. Hatred will increase (Matthew 24:10). Although we have prejudice among the races today, people during the Tribulation will hate each other because of their religion, accomplishments, and wealth, as well as heritage. There will be false prophets (Matthew 24:11) and increased wickedness as people turn their backs on all moral law (Matthew 24:12). Anarchy will reign supreme.

The Antichrist will stand in "the holy place" (Matthew 24:15). That, of course, refers to the temple in Israel. One day the temple will be rebuilt so it will be ready during the Tribulation. The Antichrist will put himself in the temple and call himself God. He will even seek to be worshiped as God (2 Thessalonians 2:3–4).

Much of the book of Revelation describes this same period of time. There are three series of judgments God will pour out upon the earth. He calls them the seal judgments (Revelation 6), the trumpet judgments (Revelation 8–9), and the bowl, or vial, judgments (Revelation 15–16).

The seal judgments are written in a scroll-like book. There are seven seals on that book, each seal covering one judgment. As the seals are broken, the judgments are read. The first judgment is a false messiah who will come. The next five judgments in order are worldwide warfare, inflation and famine, death, martyrdom, and many natural disasters in the Sun, Moon, stars, and Earth.

When the seventh seal is broken in Revelation 8:1, the seven trumpet judgments begin. This is because the seventh seal contains all the trumpet judgments. There is a telescopic effect, meaning that the seventh seal encompasses the trumpet judgments and the seventh trumpet includes the bowl judgments. In other words, when the seventh trumpet is blown, the bowl, or vial, judgments begin.

What are the trumpet judgments? The first will be a judgment on the vegetation systems of the earth. Next the transportation arrangement will be affected. Then, earth's sanitation order will be stricken. Then the heavenly bodies, the sun, moon, and stars, will be maligned. The fifth will be a judgment of pestilence. This means a horde of demonic locusts will torment the peoples of the earth. Finally, the sixth trumpet will be a judgment of death.

The bowl, or vial, judgments are the last series of judgments to come down during that time (Revelation 15–16). Today, when we say that our cup is full, we mean that our cup of blessing is full. One day, however, God's cup, or bowl, of judgment will be full, and He will cast it down upon the earth.

The bowl judgments are climactic judgments. The first will be malignant sores that come upon those who have the mark of the Beast (the number 666 on the right hand or forehead). The next one will smite the seas. The third will affect the rivers of the earth. The following bowl judgment will scorch people with great heat. The fifth will send darkness upon the earth. The sixth will be when the Euphrates River dries up. Finally comes the seventh one, which will be widespread destruction.

Many believe that the Tribulation period is the seventieth week of Daniel (Daniel 9:27). When the Bible uses the term "week" in that passage, it means a group of seven years. If those judgments occur during just seven years, look what will happen with just two of them. With the fourth seal judgment, one-fourth of the population of the earth will die (Revelation 6:8). Then, under the sixth trumpet judgment a third of the people left will be killed (Revelation 9:15). In other words, under just two of the judgments, nearly half of the population of the world will be annihilated.

This is exactly what Jesus meant when He said there would be "great distress." It is the time God will pour out His greatest wrath upon the earth. When you consider the plagues in history, or the wars, or even epidemic scourges like AIDS, you can imagine how terrible this seven-year period will be. Moreover, as the Tribulation proceeds, the judgments will come with greater frequency. In other words, were the Tribulation not stopped, the entire population of the earth would be killed.

Jesus said, though, that this time will be divinely interrupted for the elect's sake (Matthew 24:22). It will be interrupted with the return of Christ to the earth to set up His kingdom here. He will stop all the judgment and subdue His enemies. He will rule the nations with a rod of iron.

We might ask the important question: Why will God allow such a time as the Tribulation period to come upon the earth? One reason is to allow the program of Satan to run its course. That is why the restrainer, who is the Holy Spirit, will be removed during that time (2 Thessalonians 2:7). (The Holy Spirit's restraining influence will be removed although He will continue to save people as He did during Old Testament times.)

Another reason is so God can again deal with the nation Israel. That nation, which means so much to the Lord, needs to learn to trust Him. During the Tribulation, Israel will be persecuted and afflicted, but many will come to Christ. A third reason is to allow God to punish those who "live on the earth" (Revelation 3:10). These are those who dwell on the earth and who have their lives wrapped up in this world and its possessions. God must deal with these people, for He must punish sin and show the world what He thinks of it.

It is important to remember that God is always a God of love. However, God is also a God of holiness, justice, and righteousness. As a holy and just God, He must judge sin righteously and thoroughly. One day He is going to rule this world as He originally wanted to rule it before the time when man first sinned. But man thought he could do a better job and has made a mess of things. Throughout the centuries we have paid the price for turning our backs on the Lord. One day, however, God will return, judge this world, and rule this earth in a time of unparalleled righteousness. The nations today are being aligned for that purpose, and God's judgment can quickly begin.

As we see the way our world is staged today, we cannot help but think that it is moving toward the day when the nations will move against each other. It is then that the judgments from God will be poured out, and Christ will come to the earth to set up His kingdom. If the catching away of the church is before that time, however, we may well sense that this day is ready to happen very soon. As we look at the events of the Tribulation period, it helps us understand which way our world is headed. We need to be living our lives daily in light of Christ's soon return.

– 8 –

THE GREAT
SNATCH

Defendant Rolando Cruz sat silently in the courtroom, just as he had in his previous exhausting trial. A helpless ten-year-old girl, home from school with the flu, was forced from her suburban Chicago home in broad daylight, raped, and murdered. Police found her badly beaten body two days later in a wooded area six miles away.

Local prosecutors presented a solid case against Cruz. Investigators firmly believed he was involved with the killing, and a statement caused by a dream proved it. Detectives said Cruz had had a vision of the murder that included details only the killer would know. The result was a guilty verdict that landed Cruz in an Illinois prison cell.

At the retrial, brought about by an effective appeal from his lawyers, Cruz listened as subject matter experts presented DNA evidence that showed he could not have been involved. Moreover, they showed he could not have made the dream statement since there was no record of it. With one stroke of the gavel, the angry judge dismissed the case, and Cruz walked out of the courtroom, a free man.

What would it be like to sit on death row for eleven years, pondering your own death by lethal injection, and then suddenly walk out of a courtroom free? What would it be like to be snatched from the piercing jaws of almost certain death?

The Bible teaches that an entire generation of people will do exactly that. The Lord will come and snatch them away to live with Him. He will take away these people in the midst of their busy lives and without any warning.

Every day you and I witness people born, then live their lives, and finally die. Some people die horrible deaths, while others die because of old age. Some die in car accidents, fires, or war. Others die because of strokes, heart attacks, or cancer. Some die quickly, while others endure long-lasting, devastating illnesses. But the fact is that all of us die.

Except for an entire generation of believers. These are not people that are better than anybody else or who have done more for society than anybody else. They are people who simply will be living at a certain time in history, a time when Christ is going to come for them. They are people who will fulfill the promise Jesus made that He "will come back and take you to be with me that you also may be where I am" (John 14:3). It is possible that you and I will be part of that unique group.

This event is commonly called the Rapture of the church. All this means is that Christ will come and snatch away a whole generation of people. He will take these people to heaven with Him. The word *rapture* is the Latin translation of the phrase "caught up" in 1 Thessalonians 4:17. One day Jesus will come to take His church to heaven.

An Old Testament prophet had a similar experience. Elijah faithfully ministered to the nation Israel. He made important God-given predictions and performed several miracles. He even defeated the prophets of a pagan god. One day when he and another prophet were walking together, God suddenly took Elijah to heaven without ever seeing death. The Bible describes this unusual event, "As they were walking along and talking together, suddenly a chariot of fire and horses of fire appeared and separated the two of them, and Elijah went up to heaven in a whirlwind" (2 Kings 2:11).

This is what will happen to an entire generation of Christians. God suddenly will take them to heaven to live with Him. They will not experience death.

Jesus described this event as He was teaching His disciples about His ascension. He suddenly announced He was going to leave them. He said, "I will be with you only a little longer. . . . Where I am going, you cannot come" (John 13:33). The One who came to be king of the world would now leave that world.

Peter could not understand Jesus' statement. The disciples had served Him faithfully for several years, and Peter thought they should head whatever coming kingdom Jesus established. But now the Head of the kingdom was leaving.

Jesus explained that although He soon would leave, believers would follow Him later. He had work to do, as did they, but He would come for them. He said, "Do not let your hearts be troubled. Trust in God; trust also in me" (John 14:1). Although we all would like to question the ways and workings of God, sometimes it is important just to obey Him. The Lord knows what He is doing and what He is going to accomplish. Sometimes our confidence must be placed in Him without wavering. What He demands is obedience.

In this context, Jesus explained why He was leaving. It was so He could prepare a proper place for those who trust Him. He said, "In my Father's house are many rooms; . . . I am going there to prepare a place for you" (John 14:2).

Jesus was describing a place built much like a large Roman house. Homes at that time were constructed foursquare with a sizable open space in the middle. The open section provided a garden that rain watered. People also used accumulated rainwater for cooking and drinking. The building surrounding the open section housed rooms used for different purposes. Some of the rooms were used for eating, others for cooking, and still others for living rooms and bedrooms.

When one of the sons married, however, he brought his bride back to the home and lived with her in a suite of rooms. This is the arrangement Jesus described to His disciples. He said that in His Father's house are many rooms, or dwelling places. There is enough space for all of us. One day He will act as a Bridegroom and bring us to the Father's house.

Jesus gave His solemn promise that He will come for us. He said, "I will come back and take you to be with me" (John 14:3). A rich man may send servants to do many things for him. However, one does not use someone else to stand in for him when he gets married. In the same way, Jesus will not send an angel or someone else for His bride but will come Himself. He spoke in terms of a wedding so that we can better picture what He meant.

The reason Jesus needed to leave was so He could "prepare" or "beautify" the rooms. He wanted to not only construct them, but also exquisitely decorate each residence. When a builder constructs a new house today and gives the owners the keys, the house is not yet a home. It takes time to hang drapes, move furniture, place pictures, and decorate the house before it looks like the home the owners want to enjoy. In the same way, Jesus is decorating our new home and making it a beautiful, exquisite place.

The book of Revelation describes this elegant home as a whole city (Revelation 21:10–22:6). It is called the "New Jerusalem" in contrast to the old city of Jerusalem, which, too, was the center of a people's life and worship. It is a charming city with walls and gates. It is foursquare and a wonderful river flows through it. It is the place that eventually will be the home of all the redeemed throughout eternity.

The important aspect of this place, however, is not only its beauty and satisfaction, but it is also the place where God dwells. Jesus said, "No one comes to the Father except through me" (John 14:6). Heaven is primarily the place where God is, and one day we will be caught up to be there with Him. This is the promise of the Rapture.

People in the early church had trouble understanding this. They wanted more details of this miracle. Some in the city of Thessalonica were afraid their friends that had already died would miss out on this wonderful event. The Lord, through an apostle, clarified exactly what would happen. Those who had died would also share in this Rapture (1 Thessalonians 4:13–18).

The apostle Paul addressed these people as "brothers" (1 Thessalonians 4:13), which shows they were one with him in having the same Savior and being part of the same universal church. He assured them that death is very real and a time for sorrow since we will not see that person again in this life. However, for those who die knowing Christ as Savior, we do not grieve as others do. The reason is that one day we will see that person in heaven, when the Rapture of the church takes place.

The wonderful prospect, however, is that these people will be raised from the dead. The reason we can believe in their resurrection is because Jesus Christ already has risen from the dead. He is the firstfruits of resurrection in that He was the first One to be raised that will never die again. If this is true for Him, then it is also true for all of those who died in this age trusting in Him as Savior.

This remarkable resurrection will occur at the time of the Rapture. When Christ comes for His church, those who have died will be raised from the dead and join those who are alive as they are snatched away to heaven. It is then that both groups, the dead and the living, will be united with Christ to enjoy Him forever.

The promise the apostle gave is so important that it came by direct authority of the Lord Himself (1 Thessalonians 4:15). Those who are alive and remain will not precede in the Rapture those who already have died. Both groups will be united to Christ at the same time.

Although the Rapture will be sudden and unannounced, a call from heaven will wake the dead and bring them out of their graves. As the apostle described it, Christ will come "with a loud command, with the voice of the archangel and with the trumpet call of God" (1 Thessalonians 4:16). As soon as that happens, the dead in Christ will be resurrected.

Resurrection is an absolute miracle of God. When a person dies, the immaterial nature, that which is inside and housed in the body, is separated from the material part, or the body itself. For one who knows Christ as Savior, the immaterial part goes immediately to be with God in heaven and the material part decays and returns to dust.

In resurrection, however, the very opposite process occurs. The body miraculously comes back together and the immaterial nature goes back as well so that the person is once again physically alive. For those who have died in Christ, they will not only be caught away to heaven physically, they also will first come back to life and be made physically alive.

When these people are resurrected, they will join an entire generation of believers that are still alive. Then, all of them together will be snatched away to meet the Lord in the air and taken back to heaven to live with Him (1 Thessalonians 4:16–17).

This is why we are to encourage each other with these words. The Rapture will be a time of joy and rejoicing, a time of comfort and hope. Although loved ones die, we look forward to the time when our Lord will come for us. At that time we will be united together with Him.

It is at the time of the Rapture that all of us will receive a new kind of body. Our physical bodies will be changed and made like our Lord's resurrected body. The apostle explained, "We will not all sleep, but we will all be changed" (1 Corinthians 15:51).

The fact that we will not all sleep shows that an entire generation of believers will never see death. In the Old Testament, this happened to two people, Enoch and Elijah. However, the Lord drew back the veil of the future and promised that believers alive when He returns will also never die. Instead, He will take them directly to heaven.

We do not know exactly what that body will be like. The best example is the body of Christ after He was raised from the dead. Jesus had a physical body, but a body that was not again subject to death. His friends recognized Him, but He did not need food to sustain Himself. Although God gave us an example of this body, we still would like to know aspects for which there are no revealed answers. For instance, how old will we appear, and how much will we know?

We are told how fast this change will take place. It is "in a flash, in the twinkling of an eye, at the last trumpet" (1 Corinthians 15:52). A flash or twinkling of an eye means this will be an instantaneous event. It will be a miracle of God, as quick as when Jesus changed water into wine or when He raised Lazarus from the dead (John 2:8–9; 11:43–44).

It will also be at the last trumpet. Although trumpets sometimes were used in times of judgment, they also were used for worship and celebration. For instance, when Joshua had people blow trumpets, the walls of Jericho fell down in an act of judgment (Joshua 6:20). On the other hand, trumpets were blown to gather the people to the feasts of Israel (Leviticus 23:23–25).

In end-time events, trumpets will be used for both judgment and celebration. The book of Revelation described seven judgments that are called the "trumpet judgments" (Revelation 8–9). In contrast, trumpets are used for celebration and victory (1 Thessalonians 4:16; 1 Corinthians 15:52). This trumpet will be at the time of victory over death, the time of the Rapture of the church.

When will the Rapture occur? Good people differ on the time of the Rapture in relation to the coming Tribulation period. Some believe that the true church, those who know Christ as their personal Savior in this age, will be snatched away after the Tribulation period is over. This is called the posttribulation position. Others hold that the church will be raptured in the middle of the Tribulation. The church will, according to this view, go through the first half but be taken out of this world before the severe events of the second half of the Tribulation begin. This is called the midtribulation position. There are many, however, who hold that the church will be taken away before the events of the Tribulation ever begin. This is called the pretribulation position.

People hold to a pretribulation Rapture for several reasons. First is because the church is promised to be kept from the wrath of God (1 Thessalonians 1:10; Revelation 3:10). Since the Tribulation is a time of wrath, it would make sense for the Rapture to occur before that time begins. Another reason is that the church is never seen in any of the Tribulation events. In fact, the word "church" is never used in Revelation 6–19, the chapters that describe the various events of the Tribulation.

All believers are to be looking for the return of Christ rather than for signs of the Tribulation. It is to Israel that will be on earth during the Tribulation that God gave signs for the end of the age. The church, however, is to look for the Savior from heaven (1 Thessalonians 1:10). Our hope is in God and our deliverance is in Him.

You and I should always be living in light of the Rapture. We do not know when it will take place. As we look at the events happening in our world today, we believe it may be very soon. But we should always be ready. The apostle believed he would be part of those then alive (1 Thessalonians 4:17), and every generation since has had that same hope. But whether God takes us by death or the Rapture, we must be faithful to Him and use every opportunity He gives us to serve Him.

– 9 –

THE FUTURE OF
THE UNITED STATES
AND OTHER NATIONS

On a twenty-seven-acre landfill in New York harbor lies a revered mecca for millions of hope-hungry foreigners. In the shadow of the Statue of Liberty, Ellis Island once processed 90 percent of all United States immigrants. Now it proudly stands as a national monument to the dreams and aspirations of all who came to this symbol of freedom.

Some of those newcomers give heartfelt testimonies as to why they came to this beacon of hope. "My dad decided he had enough of poverty," confides one from Italy. "With eight children, he wanted them to have a better home, a better life, and America was known as the Land of Opportunity."

A Swedish immigrant says, "I wanted to go to America because my grandmother, who I lived with, was saying, 'If I was a young girl, I'd go to America.'"

A German newcomer declared that "the difference between Germany and America was felt right off. The superintendent in the management office used to call me by my first name. They said, 'Ralph!'—for Rolf. In Germany, they would never have called me by my first name, no matter how well they knew me. Always Becker, not Ralph. And I thought, 'Well, this is democracy. That is what democracy represents'" (Peter Coan, *Ellis Island Interviews*, New York: Facts On File).

People come to the United States for many reasons. Some flee persecution, others join relatives, still others follow a dream. Perhaps the underlying reason is best expressed in the familiar words at the base of the Statue of Liberty: "Give me your tired, your poor, your huddled masses yearning to breathe free." The Statue of Liberty holds out her torch, beckoning to the masses from around the world. And people have come in droves to this "land of opportunity."

All countries, however, have problems. America struggles inwardly with vacillating levels of productivity, inflation, and moral relativism. Outwardly there are threats from other nations. "America must be great again," politicians proclaim. And some people echo, "We need to lead the world!"

Where, though, is the United States going? What is the future of this great country? Where do America and other nations fit into Bible prophecy?

As we approach end-time events, four confederacies of nations will surround the nation of Israel. Is it possible the United States will align with one of those confederacies? Or will she dominate the world, or possibly even be destroyed? Does the Bible give any indication about the future of the United States?

Some, in reading Scripture, believe certain passages may allude to the United States. A careful examination, however, shows that such conclusions are remote. For instance, they hold that the "young lions" (Ezekiel 38:13 KJV) and "distant shores" (Psalm 72:10) refer to England's colonies, namely America. A careful check, however, indicates that those are villages or shores of Tarshish, the area of southern Spain (cf. Jonah 1:3).

Others find America to be the "great eagle" (Revelation 12:14) or the "land shadowing with wings" (Isaiah 18:1 KJV). But the logical interpretation of this Revelation passage is that this is the speed with which the woman flees into the wilderness, not that this is a separate nation. The Isaiah passage refers to a nation with "whirring wings" (Isaiah 18:1), most likely a reference to the insects of Ethiopia, not aircraft of the United States.

Still others find America destroyed in the judgments that will be poured out during the Tribulation (Revelation 6:8; 8:7), or as part of the 144,000 that will come upon the earth during that time (Revelation 7). A careful study shows that the judgments in Revelation will be upon the "whole world" (Revelation 3:10), not just on one part of the earth or one nation. Moreover, the 144,000 will be a limited number of saved Jews that will be special evangelists during that time (Revelation 7:3–4). The United States does not fit these descriptions.

To say the United States is not mentioned in Scripture, however, does not mean this nation will be destroyed. When you think about it, you see that the Bible is discussing the nation Israel and what will happen around that nation during end-time events. Since the United States is not anywhere near Israel, it is logical that it is not mentioned. This is not surprising, since no other nation in the Western Hemisphere or Australia is singled out.

What, then, will happen to the United States? Certainly we can assume that when Russia comes down against Israel to take the "spoil of the land" (Ezekiel 38–39) the United States will oppose it. Perhaps Russia's actions in the Balkan States and the Middle East are setting the stage for this.

During end times there will be power shifts to the Middle East and the confederacies that surround Israel. This also includes the ten-nation revived Roman Empire, or the New Europe. Already we can see such power shifts beginning.

Then, too, there is a great redistribution of wealth to Arab nations because of the necessary oil commodity. In fact, billions of dollars from industrialized nations are pouring into the Middle East. Japan imports nearly 100 percent of its oil. Europe and the United States also import a great deal. The OPEC (Organization of Petroleum Exporting Countries) nations are rapidly accumulating vast wealth. Whole cities are built in the desert because of this money, and sophisticated weapons are making that part of the world a center of military might.

Power continues to move to the nation blocs that will one day surround Israel in end-time events. Even though there are economic problems in Russia, other nations continue to fear their missiles and internal turmoil. The economic expansion of China may mean a shift of power to the "kings of the East." Egypt continues to enjoy a leadership role among the Muslim nations, although Iranian fundamentalism is challenging this. And the rise of the Common Market is surprising when viewed against the divisive history of European nations.

Since these power shifts have begun, why is the United States still the dominant country of the world? Why does this country continue to exert such important world leadership?

Perhaps the answer lies in its technological achievements, like computers, software, and telecommunications. Other countries, such as England, Japan, and Germany, have made great strides in technology, yet they do not exert the same world leadership as does the United States. Perhaps it is our political system. However, other countries with strong political systems—like Britain, Canada, and Australia—do not have the same influence as does the United States.

When we turn from outward achievements to conditions of the heart, we get a much different perspective. The moral condition of the United States is rather dismal. Every nation has problems, but America seems to tolerate moral problems in every level of society. As a result, we might ask, "Why has God not judged this nation?" We see the breakdown of the family, the rise of abortion, homosexuality, drugs, and even shootings in schools. We could well inquire, "Why is America a leader at all?"

Centuries ago the Bible spoke to this very issue. Within its pages it tells the secret for national success. Because America has followed some of those basic principles, we live in a great nation. But will the dominance of this country continue? Or are new power shifts going to crescendo in the days ahead?

The biblical principles for national survival are strategic. First is the importance of righteousness. God said it is righteousness that "exalts a nation, but sin is a disgrace to any people" (Proverbs 14:34). The psalmist also expressed this principle: "Blessed is the nation whose God is the Lord" (Psalm 33:12).

History records that this nation was founded on basic biblical principles—it was founded on righteousness. From our coinage, which says "In God We Trust," to our Pledge of Allegiance, to the Constitution, religious freedom was the hallmark of this nation.

But today we are getting away from our founding faith. And as God said that "sin is a disgrace to any people," He easily could destroy this nation because of its sin. Did He not do that with Sodom and Gomorrah (Genesis 18–19) and the nations of Canaan (Deuteronomy 9:4–5)? How important it is for our nation and every nation to get back to God's righteousness!

There is another reason God blessed this nation. It is because of our relationship to the Jews. God told Abraham that He would "bless those who bless you, and whoever curses you I will curse" (Genesis 12:3). Although some claim that this promise has gone out of existence, they freely admit that the promise of the rest of the verse, that "all peoples on earth will be blessed through you," continues. Certainly then, God's blessing for those who bless Israel continues as well.

Throughout the history of the United States, this nation has opened its heart to Jewish people. We've provided a haven for many. Jewish people came to this country so they could worship in religious freedom. Many have found unusual opportunities in government, business, and communications. Although some other countries persecuted Jewish people in various ways, this nation has treated them better than did most others.

Furthermore, the United States had an important part in founding the modern state of Israel. Even though all that the state of Israel does is not necessarily right, the United States has consistently sought to help that nation and work with it. The United States has helped in peace negotiations and in providing the money and manpower for Middle East peacekeeping operations.

But the United States wants to keep the oil flowing. So the question is: Will this nation continue to treat equally the Jewish people and back the state of Israel? We certainly need oil since we import much from the Middle East. We also need the friendship of Arab people. The Bible promises that they also have a wonderful future under the hand of God (Isaiah 19:19–25). But as a nation we dare not move away from our support of the Jewish people or the state of Israel, even though there may be honest differences between two sovereign states. Until our Lord returns, we need to continue genuine support for this and all peoples of the world.

Perhaps the most important reason God has blessed this nation is because of the church. It is during this age that God is building His church. This means He is saving people and adding them to the body of Christ (Matthew 16:18). The major reason the Lord has not as yet returned for His church is that it is not yet complete. He has delayed His coming so that many in this age will be saved (2 Peter 3:9, 15). During this time, God's program of building His church takes precedence over dealing with the affairs of nations. One day, however, the church will be complete. When that happens, He will return for it.

The church in the United States has had a large part in being the instrument God has used for bringing people to Christ throughout the world. The United States, with only 7 percent of the world's population, has produced over 50 percent of the manpower and money for world missions. Many of the largest and most influential missionary organizations, both denominational and nondenomi-national, are headquartered in the United States.

From the human side, when we look at the moral degeneracy of our nation, we wonder why God has not as yet judged this na-tion. But from the divine side, when we look at what God is doing through the church both here and around the world, we can see why God's hand of blessing is upon this country.

One day, however, the Lord is going to come and take His true church, all those who know Christ as their own personal Savior, out of this world. Jesus said, "I will come back and take you to be with me that you also may be where I am" (John 14:3). Jesus Christ is coming again, and He is coming for His church!

What will happen when the Lord takes all true believers to be with Him? What will happen when God removes the church from the United States? No longer will there be the penetration of soci-ety with the gospel. No longer will there be restraint from sin. No longer will this nation support the Jews. And no longer will there be a world missionary enterprise led and supported by the church in this country.

All of a sudden, with the church gone, this nation will become as any other nation. All of a sudden this country will be as any oth-er group of people.

It is possible that after Christ comes for His church, this nation will then be destroyed. It is more likely, however, that the United

States will become an associate nation with one of the confederacies surrounding Israel in end-time events. The most likely candidate is the western confederacy that will be led by the Antichrist. It is that confederacy that will "devour the whole earth" (Daniel 7:23) so that no nation, including this one, can be kept in complete isolation from these events. As a result, the United States will be associated with that confederacy. This makes sense since throughout history our national ties were connected to Europe.

With the church gone, there will then be a complete power shift to the nations of the Middle East and the confederacies that surround Israel. No longer will the United States be a world power. Rather, it is set to play its part in end-time events, supporting the Man of Sin and eventually moving against Israel and the nations of the world in the war of Armageddon. It is then that Christ will come to the earth and put all enemies under His feet. This includes His enemies in this country. It is then He will judge the nations of the world. And it is then that He will rule the nations with a rod of iron, and of His kingdom there will be no end.

You and I should be involved in God's program for this age. This is the program where God is building His church. Already there are power shifts beginning, power shifts to the Middle East and power shifts to the confederacies that will surround Israel. One day God will deal with those nations and move them to carry out His purposes. But until He takes us out of this world, His purpose in this age is saving people and building His church, not building nations. We need to be God's instruments to help with His program before it is too late.

— 10 —

ANOTHER NEW MILLENNIUM

On an isolated island in the middle of the Atlantic Ocean lies a near-perfect past civilization. The rulers there built temples, palaces, harbors, and docks. People brought goods to the kings from all over the world. Animals, flowers, fruits, and vegetables flourished in the land. The country provided everything that was needed. This included *orichalcum*, a metal more precious than gold.

A large temple occupied the center of the island and had a silver exterior and a gold wall that surrounded it. A great altar stood inside and gold statutes of ten kings and their wives were placed throughout the temple. Individual palaces were as spectacular as the temple and had hot and cold springs. Baths were provided for the kings and citizens, as well as for the horses and cattle.

There were many special laws in this community. One of the most important laws mandated loyalty to the state. No fighting was permitted among citizens, and everyone was required to come to the aid of the king in the event of a coup or other effort to topple the government. The people decided about going to war and other matters, and the royal house did not have the power of life and death over any citizen unless all the kings agreed on a capital punishment verdict.

This is the story a Greek philosopher told of *Atlantis*, a distant land located west of the known world and beyond the Strait of Gibraltar. Some believe it was an eighth continent. Others think it was buried in its namesake, the Atlantic Ocean, while still others felt it was complete fiction. Plato, however, taught its existence as the ideal society of true and virtuous quality.

Throughout history, many dreamed of a better world—a place of economic prosperity, justice, and moral integrity. Many people seek a utopia, a place where everything is perfect. Plato worked out a whole arrangement for a near-perfect society, including religious and governmental life.

The Bible, however, portrays a golden age somewhat different than most people envision. It will be a world with complete justice, righteousness, and peace. It will be a place with economic prosperity and moral integrity. It will be a commonwealth where everyone will practice the same religion, and every day will include worship. It will have one supreme King, and that King will rule the entire world with righteousness and peace.

What is especially interesting is that this righteous age will be a thousand years long. It will be a whole millennium in duration, and it is not in the past, nor a dream in someone's mind, but as true as the events of Christ's birth, death, and resurrection. Furthermore, it may actually interrupt this current millennium and begin at any time. This is why we need to prepare for it, be ready to receive it, and know the events that will lead up to it. In spite of other dreams and wishes for a better world, God has a plan, and His plan is specific and always best.

Our world is facing poverty and suffering on every continent. We witness urban decay, family disintegration, environmental pollution, and moral degeneracy. We see society ravaged by jealousy and hate, greed and thievery, drugs, and murders. Materially, we are enamored with gadgets and technological advances and a world that is moving ahead, but morally we see it is falling apart.

Some believe science, psychology, or medicine can solve these problems. Others think money is the answer. Many believe more education can rid us of our negative behaviors and habits. Some hold that a new Microsoft, Intel, or the Internet will help. But as yet, none of these has moved the world toward a better, moral world. Nor will they.

The fact is that man himself must be changed before society can be changed. There must be a new heart within, a change from the inside out. It is by regeneration, not reformation, that answers are brought to the problems of life. One day God will bring into being His own perfect world, His glorious kingdom here upon this earth. Not until then will these goals fully be realized, and no counterfeit method by man will speed the process.

When will this new millennium occur? It will happen when Christ returns to the earth and sets up His kingdom here. He will arrive on a white horse and slay all His enemies. He will judge the world in righteousness and establish a government upon this earth. He will rule this world as He originally meant to rule it until sin entered it and made such rule impossible.

God's Word describes Christ's coming. He will arrive on a white horse, white being the symbol of purity (Revelation 19:11). He will be called "Faithful and True," the One who alone is consistent and conforms to reality. It is in righteousness that He will judge and wage war. That is why He must put all enemies under His feet.

Christ's eyes will also be seen as flames of fire, showing His wisdom and discernment (Revelation 19:12). On His head will be many crowns, for He is the Sovereign of the universe. Jesus' robe is dipped in blood, which not only shows His redemption for sin but His coming judgment upon the earth. His name will be the "Word of God" (Revelation 19:13). This means a disclosure or revelation, and will show He is the manifestation of God Himself.

Following Him from heaven will be His armies, the saints of God who He already has rewarded. He will smite the nations with His sharp sword (Revelation 19:15), and He will rule them with a rod of iron. He will tread the winepress of the fierce wrath of God.

Both on His robe and on His thigh, the place of strength, Christ will have a name written: "KING OF KINGS AND LORD OF LORDS" (Revelation 19:16). He is the King of all Kings and the Lord of all Lords. He is the One who not only has authority to rule but will also use that authority in ruling the world. Jesus Christ is coming again, and He is coming to set up His righteous kingdom upon this earth.

The reign of Christ will be unlike anything we know today. First, it will have a political arrangement. That has many implications. For instance, it will be an earthly kingdom. It will be a display of God's authority over all the earth (Psalm 2:8).

When God made this world, He intended to rule it, but He gave man the privilege of choice. Man thought he could do a better job and usurped God's authority. Man wanted his own human government, with kings and rulers and leaders. But now he finds that this really does not work. One day Christ will be King and rule this world as God originally intended.

During that future time Jerusalem will be exalted among the cities of the earth (Isaiah 2:2–3; Micah 4:1–2; Zechariah 14:10). That is why the city of Jerusalem is in such contention today. One day it will be chief among the cities of the earth, and the nations of the world will stream to it. During that time many people will say, "Come, let us go up to the mountain of the Lord, to the house of the God of Jacob. He will teach us his ways, so that we may walk in his paths" (Isaiah 2:3). It is from Zion, the city of Jerusalem, that the law and word of God will go forth to the whole world.

God also will judge the nations. His judgment is righteous and His decisions just. Immediate acts of sin will cause people to die immediately. It will be a time of continual peace. Swords will be hammered into plowshares and spears into pruning hooks (Isaiah 2:4). The weapons of war will be turned into implements of peace. Nations will not lift up swords against nations anymore, nor will military experts teach the art of war.

During the millennial kingdom there will be many different spheres of authority. Today, we have senators, representatives, and presidents, prime ministers and legislators—all with different governmental responsibility. So it will be in the future. Jesus Christ will be the center of His rulership. But others will serve with Him.

The church will rule with Christ (2 Timothy 2:12). Princes and elders will have an important place (Isaiah 32:1; Jeremiah 30:21), and rulers will reign with justice (Isaiah 32:1). Other leaders will govern righteously (Ezekiel 45:8–9).

Israel, the special nation chosen by God, will have a noteworthy place in the kingdom with Christ reigning on David's throne (Isaiah 9:6–7). Israel will be in the kingdom and pay allegiance to

Christ. The nation will rule over its oppressors (Isaiah 14:1–2; 61:6–7). Israelites will be called the priests of the Lord and eat the wealth of the nations. Instead of shame, they will have a double portion from the Lord during that time. God's hand will be upon them.

Israelites also will be special witnesses of God. They will speak forth as ministers of the earth (Isaiah 61:6). They will be like dew from the Lord giving forth His Word (Micah 5:7). The Lord will bless them as they serve Him.

The other nations of the earth will also enjoy an important place. They will share in the economic and spiritual blessings of God. They will be in the land and provided for there (Isaiah 14:1–2; 49:22–23; 61:5–9).

For instance, God will give the Egyptians and Assyrians a special blessing (Isaiah 19:16–25). Travel between Egypt and Assyria will be possible on a special highway built for them. They, along with the Israelites, will worship God together. God said, "Blessed be Egypt my people, Assyria my handiwork, and Israel my inheritance" (Isaiah 19:25).

Spiritual life during this time will be wonderful. Since Christ is reigning, His glory will be manifested throughout the earth (Psalm 72:19). Knowledge will never be omniscient but will continually increase. The entire earth will be full of the knowledge of the Lord (Isaiah 11:9). People, from the least to the greatest, will know God and will serve Him (Jeremiah 31:34). No longer will people need Bible teachers, for they already will know God.

God's righteousness will flourish during that time (Psalm 72:7). It is the belt about His loins (Isaiah 11:5). People will not need to make judgments, but rather the Lord Himself will judge righteously.

Another mark of this time is the joy that will come to the people of the earth. It is not a synthetic joy but a real joy of grateful hearts. The citizens will happily do their tasks like drawing water (Isaiah 12:3). They will give thanks to the Lord (Isaiah 12:4). They will shout for joy over their portion (Isaiah 61:7). They will serve because they want to do so, not because they have to. It will be an exciting time because all will have an inner desire and motivation to please God.

The Holy Spirit also will be poured out upon the world in this golden age. God promised that He will pour out His "Spirit on the house of Israel" (Ezekiel 39:29). He said that when that occurs the people will prophesy and dream dreams (Joel 2:28–29). Although the Holy Spirit is present in all believers today, during that age there will be a special outpouring of Him.

Since Christ will slay all His enemies when He comes to set up His kingdom, His reign will begin with only saved people (Ezekiel 20:33–39; Matthew 25:31–46; Revelation 19:11–21). However, the people will have natural bodies and bear children. The babies born will, as in every age, be born in sin. This is why salvation Will be needed during that time. God showed that even with a perfect environment, there will be still sin. It is not money, education, or the environment that saves. Salvation is found only in Jesus Christ. If people commit great acts of sin, however, God will immediately judge them and they will die. Jesus Christ will rule in righteousness, and He will judge sin immediately.

God also will deal with Satan, His archenemy. Satan is the one who will empower the Antichrist during the Tribulation period. During the Millennium, however, Satan will be bound and placed in the Abyss (Revelation 20:1–3). Nevertheless, he is not destroyed. After the Millennium, he will be cast into a lake of burning sulfur (Revelation 20:10).

At the end of the thousand-year period, Satan will be loosed from the Abyss for a short time. When that happens, he will incite the people who were born in sin during the Millennium and who hardened their hearts against God to rebel openly against God (Revelation 20:8). This shows that even during such a perfect age as the Millennium, sinners will turn against God. Salvation is found only in Jesus Christ, not the environment. Finally, God will take Satan and cast him into the lake of burning sulfur.

The earth itself will be affected. When God created man, He gave him dominion over this world (Genesis 1:28). However, when man sinned, God had to curse the earth, or the earth would have had dominion over man (Genesis 3:17). During the Millennium, God will lift partially the curse from the earth, and the desert will blossom as a rose (Isaiah 35:1–2). Although the lamb and the wolf will lie down together, the serpent continues to crawl on its belly (Isaiah 65:25).

Then, too, people will be born in sin. As a result, the curse will be only partially lifted during the Millennium, but is completely lifted when the new heavens and new earth are created.

During the Millennium, there will be abundant rainfall, a sign of God's blessing upon the earth (Isaiah 30:23; 35:7). There will be enough food and cattle for the whole earth (Isaiah 30:23–24). No longer will famine be the order of the day. It is then that even the animal kingdom will be at peace (Isaiah 65:25).

There will be general prosperity during the Millennium. The land will produce plenty (Ezekiel 34:25–27; Joel 2:21–27; Amos 9:13–14). There will be just compensation for work done upon the earth (Isaiah 65:21–25; Jeremiah 31:5).

During that time there will be abundant health and healing, a mark of God's grace and blessing upon this world (Isaiah 29:18; 35:5–6; 61:1–3; 65:20; Jeremiah 30:19–20; Ezekiel 47:22).

God's way is always the best way. One day Jesus Christ is coming to this earth to rule it. When He does, it will be a time of righteousness, peace, prosperity, and blessing. The answer to the struggles the world now faces is the return of Jesus Christ.

Good people differ on the time of Christ's return in relation to the Millennium. Some hold that the thousand-year period comes first, and then, after that golden age is over, Christ will return. This view is called *postmillennialism* since Christ will come *after* or *post* this period of time.

The event that will begin the Millennium, in this view, will not be Christ's return but rather the gradual improvement of society. This will be accomplished either through environmentalism or reconstructing society in such a way that only Christians are in leadership roles. This means that we should vote only for Christians, and use services only owned and operated by Christians. In this way, we can establish a Christian society and get back to the laws of the Bible, especially the Old Testament Law.

This view was especially popular during the end of the 1800s when Darwinian evolution was applied to eschatology. However, it is again becoming popular as many hold that Christians need to reconstruct society along Christian principles.

Another popular view regarding the Millennium is *amillennialism*. This view holds that the Millennium is not really a literal thousand-year period, but rather encompasses the whole present age. This view holds that we should view the prophetic portions of Scripture not in any literal sense, but only as symbols of what the biblical writers envisioned. After this present age, we should expect the return of Christ and then one large general judgment. In this view, the church is now enjoying the spiritual aspects of God's promises to Israel, and Christ is now sitting on David's throne in heaven ruling the earth. We, therefore, should not look for any future thousand-year reign of Christ, only a spiritual future state.

A third view of the Millennium is called *premillennialism*. This view holds that Christ's return is *pre* or *before* the Millennium. It holds that the prophetic portions of Scripture should be interpreted in a literal sense, exactly like the other parts of Scripture. When one does this, he finds that Scripture makes perfect sense. Prophetic portions of books like Daniel, Isaiah, Matthew, Peter, and Revelation place Christ's return before the thousand-year Millennium begins. The Millennium is the time of Christ's reign upon this earth and will demonstrate to the world what a righteous government is like. This is why this author takes this position.

Although the views of the relationship of the church to the Tribulation, previously discussed, sound similar to these millennial views, they are different. They are views concerning the Tribulation (post, mid, and pretribulationism), the time period immediately before Christ comes to set up His kingdom. These views of the Millennium concern whether or not this thousand-year period is literal and whether Christ will return before or after it.

What should we be doing until our Lord returns? We need to communicate the gospel to the world and demonstrate the Christian life by the way we live our lives. It is as others see visible examples of the life of Christ that they will accept God's provision for them. When they do, they, too, can look forward to the time when Christ returns, first for His church, and then to set up His kingdom upon this earth. They can look forward to His righteous reign upon this earth.

11

ONE MINUTE AFTER DEATH

In a hectic hospital emergency room on a plain, sheet-covered gurney lies a ninety-three-year-old woman, still breathing, but barely. The intern makes a quick examination, orders tests, and instructs that the oxygen flow increase. After he views the EKG, he calls for the surgeon.

This lady suffered a heart attack, and the paramedics got her to the hospital just in time. An emergency surgical team assembles and inserts a pacemaker, but half the heart is shut down. Angioplasty, the opening of an artery with a balloon, is also performed. What this woman really needs, however, is a heart bypass operation, but this medical staff does not recommend that operation for a person this age. Death is only a matter of time.

People die every day, in fires, floods, accidents, illnesses, and a myriad of other ways. Seldom do we think about it or give it a second thought. But when the person is your mother, father, grandmother, grandfather, son, daughter, or other relative, your attention is riveted to the situation.

Everybody wants to know the details of dying, even though few are willing to say so. We would like to understand what happens to a stricken relative and even anticipate the specifics of our own demise. However, the nature of death, for most, remains a secret, filling us with both fascination and fear.

Deep inside, no normal person really wants to die. Yet Scripture says that "man is destined to die once, and after that to face judgment" (Hebrews 9:27). Although no one looks forward to death, this is a subject everyone contemplates sooner or later. Death is coming to all of us, and it is important that we be prepared.

People have held many different views about life after death throughout history. For instance, the Egyptians believed their kings would live in the next world much as they did here. As soon as a king began his reign, his subjects would begin building his tomb. When he finally died, many of his earthly possessions were buried in the tomb with him.

Others believe that death is the end of all things. They think man is an animal and when death comes, he ceases to exist. This life is all there is; there is no life after death. Such a view, of course, is in conflict with Scripture. The Bible teaches that one day all will be raised to eternal existence (John 5:28–29).

Still others believe in soul transmigration. This is the view that after death, the immaterial nature of the person goes into another person or even an animal. Sometimes this is called reincarnation. The person is believed to come back as someone or something else. But again there is no scriptural basis for such a view. The Bible shows that each individual is personally accountable after death (Luke 16; Revelation 4). Man does not float from body to body.

People also hold to conditional immortality. This view is that those who do good works in this life have a life after death. However, those who do evil works will cease to exist after death. In other words, those who live good, noble, and moral lives will be rewarded with an afterlife. Otherwise, they disappear. Scripture again does not support this view. Jesus said that even the wicked come out of the tombs (John 5:28–29). With no afterlife, how can those who were wicked all their lives be truly punished?

Some believe in universalism. This is the view that everybody will live with God in heaven. There is no hell, only a place of eternal peace and bliss. This view also is in conflict with Scripture. The

Bible teaches that there is a heaven and a hell. Not everybody is saved. Only those who have trusted Christ as their own Savior from sin will live with Him forever.

Although individuals may disagree on the details, many believe there is life after death. This is because only with a future life can moral aspirations adequately be fulfilled. Many aspire to worthy goals that are never accomplished. Having a future life could mean continuing with those goals and seeing them realized. Good works may continue forever.

Another reason for needing a future existence is because of the nature of rewards. Have you ever considered how a person who is wicked all his life can truly be punished? Or how a person who has done great and noble things all his life can truly be rewarded? For instance, what about a man who kills thirteen people? Although he is tried and convicted of murder, he can die only once for that particular crime. How, then, can he truly be punished for such behavior? The only answer is that there must be life after death. There must be a future existence in which people are properly punished or rewarded.

The best reason, however, for needing a future existence is in the Scriptures. Throughout the Bible God shows that we will be resurrected from the dead and that there is life after death. For instance, the book of Job, probably the oldest book of the Bible, says so. Job not only knew his Redeemer lived but also knew that "after my skin has been destroyed, yet in my flesh I will see God; I myself will see him with my own eyes—I, and not another" (Job 19:26–27). If Job one day would see God, he would have to have a future conscious existence.

When we turn to the Bible, we also begin to understand what life after death involves. The various writers of Scripture assure us it involves resurrection. For instance, the Old Testament prophet Daniel taught there was life after death. He said that Israel would come forth from the grave (Daniel 12:1–2). The prophet Isaiah also spoke of life after death (Isaiah 26:19).

Jesus, however, helped us understand some important facts of the resurrection. He proclaimed He was the source of life. One day, He said, "all who are in their graves will hear his voice and come out" (John 5:28–29). He promised that everyone would live again after death.

He also helped us see that there will be two kinds of resurrection. Although all will come forth from the graves, all will not have the same place in eternity. For instance, Jesus said there will be one resurrection for those who do good (John 5:29). This means to do good as God sees good. It is accepting His provision from sin, accepting Christ as one's personal Savior. Only those who know and trust Christ will be raised from the dead in the first kind of resurrection (cf. Revelation 20:6).

The second type of resurrection will be for those who do evil. This will be the resurrection of condemnation or judgment (John 5:29). The ones who do evil are the ones who do not accept Christ as Savior from sin. They are the ones who do not do good as God sees it. They will be raised from the dead, however, but they will not be in the same place as believers.

Although the unsaved have eternal existence, they will not be eternally with the Lord. They will be separated from Him and cast into the lake of burning sulfur. For them, this will be the second death (Revelation 20:14).

The New Testament also helps us understand when these resurrections will take place. For instance, the first type of resurrection will occur in several different stages, or phases, rather than all at once. This means that people who lived in different ages, or time periods, will be raised in their specific group. However, all of these people together will form one large group in that they all will have part in the first kind of resurrection, the resurrection of life.

The first one raised in this type of resurrection was Jesus Christ. He is the firstfruits of resurrection (1 Corinthians 15:23). This means He was the first One raised never to die again. Although others, such as Jairus's daughter, the woman of Nain's son, and Lazarus, were raised, they died again. Jesus Christ was raised never to die.

The next group to be raised in the resurrection of life will be the church. This group will be raised at the Rapture, Christ's coming for His church (1 Thessalonians 4:16–17). Although there are many years between the resurrection of Christ and that of the church, both groups are part of the first kind of resurrection. The type is the same, but the time of their resurrection is different.

A third group that will be raised as part of the first resurrection is the Tribulation saints. This group consists of those who will die during the Tribulation period and know Christ as Savior. Many of them will be martyred during the Tribulation for their faith and testimony. They will be raised at the second coming of Christ. This is the time immediately after the Tribulation when Christ will come to set up His kingdom here on earth (Revelation 20:4).

Another group that will be part of this resurrection is the Old Testament saints. These are those who were saved during Old Testament times. These people will be raised when Christ comes to set up His kingdom on the earth. This is the same time as when Tribulation saints will be raised (Daniel 12:1–2).

The second resurrection, the resurrection to judgment, is another story. All involved in this resurrection will be raised at one time. After their resurrection, they will stand before the Great White Throne Judgment and then are cast into the lake of burning sulfur (Revelation 20:11–15). This is why this is called the resurrection to judgment or the resurrection of condemnation.

This Great White Throne Judgment will occur right after the Millennium, the thousand-year reign of Christ upon the earth. Somewhere between heaven and Earth there is a great white throne. The symbol white is used, for it signifies God's holiness, purity, and sinless character. Christ Himself will be the Judge, and the unrighteous will assemble before Him.

At this judgment, two sets of books will be opened and examined. The first set of books will be the Lamb's Book of Life (Revelation 20:12). This is the list of all who trusted Christ as Savior. None of the names of those standing before the Lord at this judgment will be found in this book.

The other set of books will be a book of works. These will be books that contain the works done by unsaved people. Certainly, if there is any basis for God to allow them to enter His heaven, it would be found here. However, works always indicate a person's faith. Scripture says that "faith without deeds is dead" (James 2:26). As a result, since the works of these people will show their true stripes and sinful condition, God cannot let them into His heaven. These books will be a double check on all those that will stand at this judgment.

The faithless works of these people show something else. They show the grace of God. When you stop to think about it, we find that God always deals with man by grace. However, man in and of himself tries to come to God by his own works. Man tries to buy his way to heaven by doing things for God or his fellowman. God's way to heaven, on the other hand, is for man to trust Him for his salvation, to accept the provision of Christ's death on the cross as the way to God. When man does it God's way, he will then do good works as a *result* of his salvation, not as a *means* to obtain it.

In this judgment, God will use man's own standard, that of works, to show he is completely lost. Man's righteous acts are like filthy rags (Isaiah 64:6). No one in and of himself is able to measure up to the righteousness God requires to enter His heaven.

Because of the Great White Throne Judgment, many results will occur. First, there will be eternal death. This does not mean man will cease to exist, but rather that there will be eternal separation from God. These people will be outside of God's presence forever. In addition, the unsaved will be cast into the lake of burning sulfur, the place of everlasting torment for the wicked (Matthew 25:41, 46). These unbelievers will be everlastingly punished for their sin.

In the meantime, all those who trust Christ as Savior during this age will stand before the Lord at another judgment. This is called the judgment seat of Christ. In contrast to the Great White Throne Judgment, it will not be a court of condemnation. Rather, it will be a place of commendation and is called such. The original word used for this judgment (*bema*, 2 Corinthians 5:10) means a judging stand, or place where people were commended for a job well done. For instance, when footraces were run near the city of Corinth, the winner would come and stand before this judging stand and receive his victor's crown. In the same way, God says that all believers in this age must stand before the judging stand of Christ and there they will be rewarded for their works.

The basis of this judgment is, first, that there is a proper foundation (1 Corinthians 3:11). That foundation is Jesus Christ and what He accomplished on the cross of Calvary for the sins of the world. He died for us, and those who accept that provision will be the ones standing here. That is why this judgment is only for believers.

The other basis of this judgment is seen by the kinds of materials that we use to build our lives for God. Six possible materials are allowed: gold, silver, costly stones, wood, hay, or straw (1 Corinthians 3:12). However, although six materials are mentioned, in reality, there are only two types. There is that which is *permanent*, that which God puts into the life: gold, silver, costly stones. And there is that which is *perishable*, that which we try to put into our own lives: wood, hay, and straw.

The basis of this judgment will be whether or not we allowed God to work through us, or whether we tried to do things in our own self-effort. Our attitude and motivation in serving God is to do only what Jesus would want us to do. To work for God, there should be right *activity* and also a right *attitude*—an attitude that puts Him first. It is because of a right attitude that believers will be rewarded when they stand before Him.

The Bible pictures the rewards believers will receive as crowns. These crowns will not be worn in a spirit of competition. Rather, they will be cast at Christ's feet in an act of worship (Revelation 4:4, 10–11). We will have done nothing to deserve them, only that we were faithful to what God wanted us to do. The great embarrassment, however, is going to come when there are those with little or nothing to offer to Him.

This judgment of commendation will take place in heaven, right after the church is raptured. It is then that believers will stand before Him and He will reward them.

Is there life after death? Although some people may not be sure, the Scriptures answer with a resounding "Yes!" There is life after death for both believers and unbelievers. But how much better to know Christ as one's Savior than to stand before Him in a future day as a condemning Judge! It is much better to be at the judgment seat of Christ than to be at the Great White Throne Judgment.

12

THERE IS A PLACE YOU CAN ENJOY FOREVER

Nestled among rolling hills and atop a lush mountain overlooking the rich blue Pacific Ocean is a unique place called "The Enchanted Hill." Here in Southern California lies the most spectacular private residence ever imagined by a human being. Kings live in palaces they inherit, but a media mogul built this castle that was the ultimate in earthly magnificence, inside and out.

William Randolph Hearst owned twenty-nine newspapers, fifteen magazines, eight radio stations, four film companies, two million acres of land, plus numerous other holdings. At the height of his wealth, he built San Simeon. He even scoured several castles in Europe and shipped over their contents in crates.

This grandiose home has one hundred forty-six rooms, including thirty-eight bedrooms, fourteen sitting rooms, thirty-one bathrooms, two libraries, a kitchen, a billiard room, a movie theatre, an assembly hall, and a dining hall. Included also are three huge guest houses, a gigantic outdoor and a number of smaller indoor pools, formal gardens, and many Greek and Roman statues. It also was home to the largest private animal zoo in the world.

Today this twenty-eight-year building effort during Hollywood's golden era, along with its opulent display of paintings, sculptures, tapestries, antique silver, and furniture, is now a California State Historic Monument open to the public.

There are a lot of beautiful homes in the world. Another, more high-tech home lies on the beautiful Lake Washington shore, near the city of Seattle. Bill Gates, CEO of Microsoft and reportedly the world's richest man, included some unique features in his home. When a visitor enters the house, an electronic pin is fastened to his clothes. Then as the person walks through the house, lights are automatically turned on, music favorites play, and movies, news, and phone calls follow him or her. Reproductions of paintings and photographs are projected on screens throughout the house according to the special interests of the guest.

What kind of home is your dream? All of us think about what we would like in a perfect home. But although there are some beautiful places on this earth, those who live there awhile generally find something wrong with them, for they are all man-made. One day, however, God is going to make a beautiful place for all believers, a place that will be the ideal, perfect home. Moreover, everything will work and nothing will ever be wrong with it.

After the Millennium, God will destroy this heaven and earth (2 Peter 3:7, 10–13). Scripture teaches that the very makeup of this world will pass away, for it has been affected by sin. It is then that God will create a new heaven and a new earth (Revelation 21:1). In fact, there will be a new kind of heavens and a new kind of earth. The geographical boundaries, however, may be similar to what we know today, but it will be a perfect heaven and earth and a place without sin.

In addition, the Lord will create a Holy City, the New Jerusalem (Revelation 21:2). This place will be the home of the redeemed of all ages. It will be a spectacular place that Scripture carefully describes.

Jesus mentioned briefly to His disciples before He left this earth that He was going back to heaven "to prepare a place for you" (John 14:2). That place is evidently the New Jerusalem, which is elaborately portrayed in the book of Revelation. When Jesus first informed His disciples of this place, He pictured it as having many rooms. He wanted them to know that although they could not come with Him then, when they would come, there would be adequate space for them. Now that place is described as a beautiful city, for God wants us to know how it will be our final home.

The name of this city is interesting. It is called "holy" since it will have in it only those who are holy, who are perfect in God's sight. It is called "new" in contrast to the present city of Jerusalem. Today's city, whose name means "city of peace," is the site of many wars throughout history. It has even been destroyed several times. Now it is the center of contention and is to endure more bloodshed in the future.

The New Jerusalem, however, is different. It will be faultless since it will be created by God. It will not be built from the earth or from the materials of the earth. Moreover, the preparation of it will be "as a bride beautifully dressed for her husband" (Revelation 21:2). Just as a bride is perfectly prepared for her husband on her wedding day, so this city will be beautifully dressed by God as it comes from Him out of heaven. Previously, Jesus was pictured as a Bridegroom coming for His bride, the church, at the Rapture. Here, the New Jerusalem will not be seen as a bride, but is carefully *dressed as a bride* is prepared for her husband. This city will be the permanent dwelling place of the saints of God throughout eternity.

The builder of this place is none other than God Himself. He is the One who will build it, and therefore it will be perfect as He is perfect (Hebrews 11:10). Abraham looked for a city. Some think he was looking for a land or a country, but he was actually looking for a city. He found a land and a country, and one day he will find this city of God. This will be the place God has for all of us who know Him.

Since the city will be so different from anything we know, the Bible pictures its beauty as a place of gold, pearls, and precious stones (Revelation 21:18–21). These materials are the most valuable treasures we can comprehend. As a result, we can only imagine the loveliness, adornment, and charm of this special place.

Around the city will be a great wall, a wall of protection and exquisite decoration (Revelation 21:17–18). It will be made of jasper, a stone that is pure crystal. Perhaps that emphasizes the preciousness of the city, its holiness as well as God's deity.

The city will have twelve foundations (Revelation 21:14). The names of the twelve apostles will be found in these foundations.

This would include Matthiass who took Judas', place (Acts 1:26). As the church is built upon the foundation of the apostles (Ephesians 2:20), so they will be memorialized in the foundations of the New Jerusalem.

The city will have twelve gates (Revelation 21:12–13). Since the city will be constructed foursquare, there will be three gates on each side of the city. The names of the twelve tribes of Israel will be in those gates. Although God deals with Israel in many different ways, here in the heavenly city will be those who are saved and who are of Israel.

Each gate will be formed of one single pearl (Revelation 21:21), symbolizing beauty, purity, and unity. An angel will be stationed at each gate to watch over those entering the city and to keep out anything that would defile the city (Revelation 21:12, 27). Angels who serve the Lord continue to serve Him throughout eternity. The gates will never be closed, so there will be free access to the presence of God (Revelation 21:25).

The streets of this city will be pure gold (Revelation 21:21). The original word translated "street" literally means "open place." It is the custom of modern cities to have malls with many open places between buildings. The same will be in the heavenly city. There is no description of any grass, but rather all the open places, the space between buildings, will be of pure gold.

What does pure gold look like? When gold is refined, it is impossible to make it completely pure. In fact, it is the impurity in gold that gives it its color. But if gold could be refined completely, in an absolutely pure form, it well may be transparent as glass. This is the way the Spirit of God describes the gold of this city (Revelation 21:21).

The illumination of the city will be the glory of God and of the Lamb. The city will have no need of any sun, stars, or other illuminating body. Rather, the glory of the Lord Himself will provide the light for the city (Revelation 21:23; 22:5).

The size of the city will be very large. It will be 12,000 furlongs, or 1,400 miles, in each direction (Revelation 21:16). Since the city will be foursquare, the base of it will be 1,400 miles, and it will be 1,400 miles high. This is a huge amount of space. It is the distance halfway across the United States. But since this city will hold the redeemed of all ages, it needs to be large.

The shape of the city may be in the form of a cube, for that geometric figure answers the description of its equal length, breadth, and height (Revelation 21:16). But a pyramid also answers that description. If it will be a pyramid, it would help us understand how the river of God could encircle it from the top to the bottom (Revelation 22:1). It would start at a very narrow base at the top, and then wind around throughout the city as it goes to the bottom. Perhaps the pyramids of Egypt foreshadowed such a city.

The people who will inhabit the city will all be believers, for nothing can enter the city that defiles it (Revelation 21:27). Moreover, all unbelievers will be in the lake of burning sulfur throughout eternity (Revelation 20:15).

God describes these city inhabitants. First, there will be an innumerable company of angels (Hebrews 12:22–24). These are good angels, those who have not sinned against God. Some of them will stand at the gates of the city. Others will continually worship God (cf. Isaiah 6; Revelation 4).

The church will also be in this city. This is the group of people who know Christ as Savior in this age. They are the ones who are called out from this world, both Jew and Gentile, and are united to the body of Christ. One day they will be caught up to be with Christ, rewarded by Him, and return with Him when He sets up His kingdom upon this earth. Their eternal abode will be the New Jerusalem.

God Himself will be in this city, and His glory will fill the place. In addition, the spirits of just men made perfect, or Old Testament saints, will inhabit the city. This is the place where Abraham and all the other Old Testament believers will live.

Jesus Himself, the Mediator of the new covenant, will be present in the city. It is the glory of the Lamb that will enlighten the city, providing light for all.

When will the city come down upon the earth? Some believe it will appear only during the eternal state, the time after the reign of Christ upon the earth. This is because it is mentioned in the book of Revelation after the millennial reign of Christ.

A careful study of this passage, however, shows there will be a tree in the city for the healing of the nations (Revelation 22:2).

Moreover, angels will be at the gates so nothing that would defile the city is allowed to enter it (Revelation 21:12, 27). Why would these conditions be needed in the eternal state?

Perhaps a better view is that this passage is describing the city from heaven, not when it will appear. If this is true, the city may appear during both the Millennium and the eternal state. During the Millennium it could come down and hover over the old city of Jerusalem. This is because in that part of the world there is not enough room geographically to house it. At the end of the Millennium, it would be taken up to heaven while this present heaven and Earth are destroyed and new ones created. Finally, it would come down upon the new earth and continue as the home of the redeemed.

This helps us better understand the Millennium. During that golden age, there will be people on earth with natural bodies who bear children. At the same time, there will be people with glorified bodies, those raptured and those resurrected. These people will dwell in the New Jerusalem, even though they would have access to the earth. Angels would then guard the gates of the city so nothing could enter that would defile it. During the eternal state, when the city would be upon the new earth, guarding angels would not be necessary.

God has a wonderful destiny for all who know Him. The place He has promised us is a place of beauty, exquisiteness, and elaborate decoration. It is a place yet to come upon the earth. But heaven is not only a place; it is also a person. It is having fellowship with God forever. It is being where He is.

You and I can now enjoy that heavenly life by enjoying His fellowship in prayer, in worship, and in joining other believers in the study of His Word. We can demonstrate the life of Christ to a world that needs to know Him. One day He will come for us and take us to be with Him. Then the day will come when we will have our eternal abiding place and enjoy it forever with the Lord. Then will be the day when "He will wipe every tear from their eyes. There will be no more death or mourning or crying or pain, for the old order of things has passed away" (Revelation 21:4).

UNDERSTANDING THE
PROPHECIES
OF THE
MILLENNIUM

STUDY GUIDE AND
SELF-CHECK QUIZZES

STEVEN J. KEMP
AND
EDGAR C. JAMES

INTRODUCTION

The following lessons are part of a Moody Bible Institute correspondence course that is wrapped around this book. However, they may also be used as an interactive study guide for individuals or groups using this book.

Enrollment in the course includes study of this book, completion of additional assignments, and evaluation by examination. In order to enroll, call 800/955-1123 or write to Moody Bible Institute, Independent Studies Customer Service, 820 N. LaSalle Blvd., Chicago, IL 60610.

INTRODUCTION TO THE STUDY OF BIBLICAL PROPHECY

The purpose of this lesson is to help you appreciate the value of biblical prophecy and prepare you for more specific study of biblical prophecies.

1. Read Chapter 1 in this book.

2. Read John 14, 2 Timothy 3, and 2 Peter 3 in the Bible so that you can see these key biblical passages in context.

3. Reread Chapter 1 in this book and look up all of the Scripture references as the author refers to them.

4. What stories have you heard about people's dramatic preparation for the end times? Have you or someone you know ever considered being involved in such an exercise? What sort of discussions do you have with others about this subject?

5. In what ways are these stories similar to each other and the stories in this chapter? What seems to draw people to them? What is missing from many of these experiences?

6. Are there concerns that you have today about events that seem to be the fulfillment of prophecy? What most worries you about the situation in which you live?

7. Does the study of prophecy lead you to the power of God, purposes of God, peace for troubled hearts, and purity of life? Why or why not? Which of these items listed in the chapter do you sense the greatest need for right now?

8. Spend a few minutes right now asking God to provide you with power, purpose, peace, and purity as you participate in this study.

Here are five true/false questions that will help you know whether you have learned the content of this chapter:

1. Only Christians plan for the end of the world.

2. The promise of Christ's return is coupled with admonition for godly living.

3. The apocalypse is a time predicted in the book of Revelation.

4. Psychics, stars, and dreams are accurate ways to determine the future.

5. There is no way to predict national or world events.

Answers to these questions are given on page 133.

LESSON 2

EUROPE AND BIBLICAL PROPHECY

The purpose of this lesson is to understand biblical prophecies regarding Europe, identify signs of their modern fulfillment, and respond appropriately as contemporary Christians.

1. Read Chapter 2 in this book.

2. Read Daniel 2, Daniel 7, and Revelation 17 so that you can see the key biblical prophecies in context.

3. Reread Chapter 2 in this book and look up all of the Scripture references as the author refers to them.

4. What have you read or heard that seems to relate to the fulfillment of biblical prophecies about Europe? Perhaps you could ask two or three fellow workers at your place of employment to discuss this with you. What has happened in the world since the writing of this book that confirms, challenges, or informs the material in this book?

5. Do the biblical prophecies about Europe mean that we should dismiss all Europeans as part of a plot to defeat Christ? Should we treat the European Common Market with disgust and avoid all interactions? What should be our attitude toward Europeans? How should European Christians respond to the things that are happening around them?

6. Are there lessons to be learned from the fact that Christianity flourished in Europe during previous centuries, but is now stagnant in many places? What parts of your Christian life are you taking for granted where you live now? What are three specific things that you might do today to help you ensure that those things won't be lost over time?

Here are five true/false questions that will help you know whether you have learned the content of this chapter:

1. The Bible predicts a confederation of countries in the same area as the Old Roman Empire.

2. The European Union Common Market is similar to the western confederacy which plays an important part in end-times events.

3. The Bible clearly identifies the nations that will make up the new Europe.

4. The common currency for the New Europe, the euro, has been in existence since World War II.

5. The Antichrist will lead the western confederacy into war against Israel.

THE ANTICHRIST AND PROPHECY

The purpose of this lesson is to understand biblical prophecies about the Antichrist, identify signs of their modern fulfillment, and respond appropriately as contemporary Christians.

1. Read Chapter 3 in this book.

2. Read Daniel 7 and II Thessalonians 2 so that you can see the key biblical prophecies in context.

3. Reread Chapter 3 and look up all of the Scripture references as the author refers to them.

4. Have you ever heard someone making claims about the identity of the Antichrist? Does someone come to your mind as a likely prospect to be the Antichrist? What about them fits the description? What doesn't fit the description? Perhaps you could ask two or three people in your church to answer these questions in order to expand your own perspective.

5. Do you think that miracles are always a sign from God? If so, do you recognize that you are susceptible to the sort of lies that will be told by the Antichrist and his followers? What other lies are being told in today's world? Which ones are most likely to deceive you or catch you off guard?

6. How should a Christian respond to increased dependence on electronic commerce? Are there other biblical admonishments or godly principles that help you know how to conduct financial activities electronically?

7. To what degree are you and others around you looking to earthly leaders to bring tranquility and prosperity to this world? In what ways could these attitudes hasten the acceptance of the Antichrist? List two or three ways in which you tend to take your eyes off God and put them on earthly leaders.

Here are five true/false questions that will help you know whether you have learned the content of this chapter:

1. In end times, the people will be so ready for world leaders, they will happily accept the Antichrist.

2. Scripture gives enough prophecy for us to identify today the exact person who will be the Antichrist.

3. The Antichrist will have an assistant called "the False Prophet."

4. The mark of the Beast will be put on the left arm or right cheek.

5. Miracles are always a sign from God.

LESSON 4

RUSSIA AND BIBLICAL PROPHECY

The purpose of this lesson is to understand biblical prophecies about Russia, identify signs of their modern fulfillment, and respond appropriately as contemporary Christians.

1. Read chapter 4 in this book.

2. Read Ezekiel 38 so that you can see the key biblical prophecies in context.

3. Reread Chapter 4 and look up all of the Scripture references as the author refers to them.

5. Does your understanding of current events in Russia match the author's applications to biblical prophecy? Perhaps you could ask two or three others in your neighborhood about their views. What other events do you know that confirm, correct, or inform your understanding of biblical prophecy regarding Russia?

5. What do you think a Russian Christian, living in Moscow, thinks about these prophecies? What would you do if you lived in Moscow and came to understand that your country seemed to be headed toward a confrontation with God Himself?

6. Given your understanding of current events, which of the reasons listed in the chapter for the world's interest in Israel do you think is most likely? Why else might a nation or ruler be interested in control or involvement in the land of Israel?

Here are five true/false questions that will help you know whether you have learned the content of this chapter:

1. Russia seems to be the chief leader of an eastern confederacy that will one day march into the Middle East.

2. Some African and Middle East countries may align themselves with the northern confederacy.

3. The Dead Sea is one of the richest chemical beds in the world.

4. The biblical prophecies that apply to Russia are found in the book of Revelation.

5. God will utterly destroy the northern confederacy.

LESSON 5

ASIA AND
BIBLICAL PROPHECY

The purpose of this lesson is to understand biblical prophecies about Asia, identify signs of their modern fulfillment, and respond appropriately as contemporary Christians.

1. Read chapter 5 in this book.

2. Read Revelation 16 so that you can see the key biblical prophecies in context.

3. Reread Chapter 5 and look up all of the Scripture references as the author refers to them.

4. Does your understanding of current events in Asia match the author's applications to biblical prophecy? Perhaps you could ask two or three people at your place of employment what they think of biblical prophecies and current events in Asia. What other events do you know that confirm, correct, or inform your understanding of biblical prophecy regarding Asia?

5. How do you see other parts of Asia, such as Korea and Indonesia, relating to China, Japan, and India?

6. Is there significance in biblical prophecy to the incredible church growth that has taken place in certain parts of Asia? Could the development of the church in Korea and China be a last chance for people in Asia to turn to Christ? What might you be able to do to support the growth of the church in this region?

Here are five true/false questions that will help you know whether you have learned the content of this chapter:

1. There are more than 1 billion people in China.

2. The exact names of the nations in the eastern confederacy are named in Scripture.

3. In terms of human resources, China has the world's largest standing army.

4. The Euphrates River forms a natural land bridge from Asia to the Middle East.

5. Many countries rely on India's oil production exports.

LESSON 6

ARMAGEDDON AND BIBLICAL PROPHECY

The purpose of this lesson is to understand biblical prophecies about Armageddon, identify signs of their modern fulfillment, and respond appropriately as contemporary Christians.

1. Read chapter 6 in this book.

2. Read Matthew 24, Revelation 14 and 16, and Daniel 11 so that you can see the key biblical prophecies in context.

3. Reread Chapter 6 and look up all of the Scripture references as the author refers to them.

4. What do many of these passages have in common in their description of Earth's final conflict?

5. Many Christians have fond feelings toward the current city of Jerusalem, especially with all of his history, archaeology, and theological significance. How do you feel about the fact that it will someday be the focus of great bloodshed?

6. Does your understanding of current events in Egypt match the author's applications to biblical prophecy? Perhaps you could discuss these prophecies and current events with someone else in your family. What other events do you or they know that confirm, correct, or inform your understanding of biblical prophecy regarding Egypt?

7. What connection do you see between Egypt and the other parts of Africa in the fulfillment of biblical prophecies regarding the king of the South?

8. How does the world come to turn against God? How can they imagine that they might win? What does this tell us about the depth of the fallenness of human beings who are already turned away from Him?

9. In your concern for Israel, how much of your hope is tied up in the role of earthly governments to protect Jerusalem? What do you understand to be an appropriate balance between political support and divine dependence?

Here are five true/false questions that will help you know whether you have learned the content of this chapter:

1. Scripture calls the world's final military campaign as "the great day of Antichrist."

2. Megiddo is located in north central Palestine.

3. Armageddon is known as the "west bank" area where many conflicts occur.

4. The Antichrist will put himself in the rebuilt Temple and call himself "god."

5. Egypt and the southern confederacy will not be active participants in Armageddon.

THE TRIBULATION AND BIBLICAL PROPHECY

The purpose of this lesson is to understand Biblical prophecies about the Tribulation, identify signs of their modern fulfillment, and respond appropriately as contemporary Christians.

1. Read chapter 7 in this book.

2. Read Matthew 24-25, Revelation 15-16, and Daniel 9 so that you can see the key biblical prophecies in context.

3. Reread Chapter 7 and look up all of the Scripture references as the author refers to them.

4. Are these passages optimistic or pessimistic about the future? As you look at the world, do you see things getting better or worse? Ask two or three teenagers for their view of current events and the condition of the world. How is your perspective informed by biblical prophecy, your own personality, or others who shape your opinions? Have you found your perspective changing over the course of your life?

5. Which of the various judgments in Revelation seem the most harsh to you? Do you struggle with why God brings such judgments? Why does He do it? How can He be in control while so much seems to be going wrong?

6. Ponder and meditate for several minutes on the suffering that Jesus Christ himself endured as judgment to take the place of these judgments for those who believe. Perhaps you could use the sacrifice of Christ, the provision of the Bible, and the coming of the Holy Spirit as evidence to an unbeliever that God is doing much to extend grace and mercy to a world that is bound for judgment.

Here are five true/false questions that will help you know whether you have learned the content of this chapter:

1. Jesus warned that crime and wickedness will increase as we approach the end of the age.

2. The murders, earthquakes, and lawlessness that are part of society show that we are now in this time of Tribulation.

3. Jesus predicted the destruction of the Jewish Temple.

4. If God did not stop the Tribulation, the entire population of the earth would be killed.

5. The Tribulation is a time for God to punish sin and show His displeasure of it.

THE RAPTURE AND BIBLICAL PROPHECY

The purpose of this lesson is to understand biblical prophecies about the Rapture, identify signs of their modern fulfillment, and respond appropriately as contemporary Christians.

1. Read chapter 8 in this book.

2. Read John 13-14 and I Thessalonians 4 so that you can see the key biblical prophecies in context.

3. Reread Chapter 8 and look up all of the Scripture references as the author refers to them.

4. Do you or anyone you know struggle with the possibility of God doing something like rapturing believers to be with Him? Have you considered the fact that He has done it before (2 Kings 2)? How does this make you feel?

5. How do you live in light of the fact that Jesus may return at any time? Do you fear being caught doing something wrong or being a poor steward? Do you have joy in anticipation of being immediately in His presence? Which perspective do you tend to have the most? How do you balance the two?

6. Does the fact of a resurrection for believers affect the way that you live and your perspective on earth's problems? To what degree are you looking for cures to all problems here and now, rather than in eternity? To what degree is your hope based on earthly solutions, rather than the ultimate redemption provided in the resurrection?

Here are five true/false questions that will help you know whether you have learned the content of this chapter:

1. The word "rapture" comes from the Latin translation of the word that means "caught up."

2. God has never before caught up a believer to be with Him without the person dying.

3. Believers who have died will be caught up to heaven with those who are alive.

4. At the rapture, all believers will receive a new kind of body.

5. The thought of an any moment return of Christ should mainly produce in us fear of being caught off guard.

LESSON 9

THE UNITED STATES AND BIBLICAL PROPHECY

The purpose of this lesson is to understand biblical prophecies about the United States, identify signs of their modern fulfillment, and respond appropriately as contemporary Christians.

1   Read chapter 9 in this book.

2. Read Genesis 12, Isaiah 19, Daniel 7, and 2 Peter 3 so that you can see the key biblical prophecies in context.

3. Reread Chapter 9 and look up all of the Scripture references as the author refers to them.

4. Have you ever heard preachers or read authors who made reference to the United States in prophecy? Did they proclaim any of the misunderstandings mentioned in this chapter? How do their claims match up to the biblical prophecies themselves and the teaching of this chapter?

5. What lessons might be learned from the observation that the United States is not mentioned explicitly in Scripture? Does it mean that God doesn't care about Americans or that Americans have no significance for the future of the world or God's plan?

6. To what degree do you think that the blessing and prominent role of America in the world has been a result of national obedience, dependence on God, and concern for Jewish people as listed in this chapter? What lessons might be applied to the United States that are based on God's longsuffering with the disobedience of nations?

7. Did you know that the demographic center of the Christian population has shifted toward Africa and Asia (and away from North America)? What evidence have you known that confirms, corrects, or informs this observation? How do you see this shift relating to biblical prophecy?

8. Do you have a tendency to think of Christianity as an American religion? List two or three ways in which your own personal experience of Christianity intertwined with American culture? What are the dangers of this? List two or three aspects of culture in other parts of the world that might help you to have a more global experience of Christianity?

Here are five true/false questions that will help you know whether you have learned the content of this chapter:

1. The United States is specifically mentioned in biblical prophecy.

2. The United States was founded on biblical principles.

3. Historically, the United States has not supported the Jewish people.

4. Power shifts to the Middle East and the confederacies that surround it have already begun.

5. God's current purpose in the world is saving people and building His church.

LESSON 10

THE MILLENNIUM AND BIBLICAL PROPHECY

The purpose of this lesson is to understand biblical prophecies about the Millennium, identify signs of their modern fulfillment, and respond appropriately as contemporary Christians.

1. Read chapter 10 in this book.

2. Read Revelation 19-20 so that you can see the key biblical prophecies in context.

3. Reread Chapter 10 and look up all of the Scripture references as the author refers to them.

4. Reflect back on your answers to the questions in Lesson 1. Did these stories include anticipation of a "Millennium?" What part does the hope of a period of peaceful prosperity play in these stories (and others that you might have thought of since you completed Lesson 1)?

5. How does the anticipation of a "Millennium" in these stories relate to biblical prophecies? Do they take seriously the whole teaching of the Bible or are they focused on a few verses or components of prophecy? List a few ways in which you may tend to emphasize one aspect of prophecy over the others?

6. What is unique about the political arrangement of the reign of Christ? From where does He rule? What are the characteristics of His kingdom? Describe the relation between the spiritual life of this reign and the joy that comes to the people of earth.

7. What is your reaction to the Bible's teaching about Satan's end? Are you concerned that God allows him to be loosed again for a short time? Why do you think God allows this?

8. To what degree are you seeking the possibility of prosperity in this age and to what degree are you anticipating the guarantee of prosperity in eternity? List two or three specific things that you are longing for in this age that are unlikely to become a reality until Christ sets up His kingdom.

Here are five true/false questions that will help you know whether you have learned the content of this chapter:

1. In the New Millennium, there is one supreme King who rules the world with righteousness and peace.

2. In the future, the city of Rome will be exalted above all other cities of the world.

3. Israel, the special nation chosen by God, will rule over its oppressors in the future.

4. During the Millennium, weapons of war will be kept in storage in anticipation of the final battle with Satan.

5. During the Millennium, the Holy Spirit will be poured out in a special way.

LESSON 11

DEATH AND BIBLICAL PROPHECY

The purpose of this lesson is to understand biblical prophecies about death and respond appropriately as contemporary Christians.

1. Read chapter 11 in this book.

2. Read John 5, 1 Corinthians 15, and Hebrews 9 so that you can see the key biblical prophecies in context.

3. Reread Chapter 11 and look up all of the Scripture references as the author refers to them.

4. Have you faced impending death yourself or with someone close to you? What did you focus on during this period? Was your experience based on biblical teaching? How might it have been different based on the teaching of this chapter? Perhaps it would be helpful to talk to a mature believer who has gone through a period of grieving and ask them about their experience. How did these truths help them? How might they have been helped had they known or believed these truths at that time?

5. What does the Bible teach about eternal rewards for earthly works? What is your own attitude toward these rewards? How do you maintain the balance between seeking eternal rewards and giving all the glory to God?

6. What are the similarities and differences between the first and second resurrections?

7. Describe your own attitude toward God's judgment. What parts bring you fear? What parts bring you encouragement? How does your own attitude toward God's judgment need to be revised in accordance with the balance of Biblical teaching?

8. As you examine your own life before God, list two or three parts that have been built with permanent materials? List two or three parts that have tended to be built with perishable materials? What specific adjustments can you make today to move from perishable to permanent materials? Who in your church can you ask for assistance with these adjustments? Make plans today to talk with them this week.

Here are five true/false questions that will help you know whether you have learned the content of this chapter:

1. Conditional immortality, the view that those who do good works in this life will have life after death, is supported by Scripture.

2. There must be a future existence in order for people to be punished properly or rewarded for what they have done in this life.

3. Old Testament prophets didn't speak of life after death.

4. The great white throne judgment and the judgment seat of Christ are the same.

5. Believers can build their lives with permanent or perishable qualities.

LESSON 12

THE NEW HEAVEN, NEW EARTH, NEW JERUSALEM, AND BIBLICAL PROPHECY

The purpose of this lesson is to understand biblical prophecies about the New Heaven, the New Earth, and the New Jerusalem, identify signs of their modern fulfillment, and respond appropriately as contemporary Christians.

1. Read chapter 12 in this book.

2. Read Revelation 21-22 so that you can see the key biblical prophecies in context.

3. Reread Chapter 12 and look up all of the Scripture references as the author refers to them.

4. Imagine what your perfect home would be like. What will be even better about the eternal home that God has promised for you?

5. Exactly what will be changed when the old is made new and holy? What parts of the transformation do you most look forward to?

6. What do you think it will be like to live with angels and God Himself in the new Jerusalem? What will be similar and what will be different? How do these things make you feel?

7. Perhaps you could explain the Bible's teaching about our eternal home to someone in need. For example, someone in a hospital might benefit from having something very good to think about. Someone struggling with stress might be able to sleep better at night by meditating on these verses. Reflect on how the sharing of these truths with someone else makes you feel. What benefits do you receive by doing so?

Here are five true/false questions that will help you know whether you have learned the content of this chapter:

1. After the Tribulation and before the Millennium, God will destroy this heaven and earth.

2. Today's Jerusalem lives up to its name as the "city of peace."

3. The Bible pictures the New Jerusalem's beauty as a place of gold, pearls, and precious stones.

4. Abraham and all the other Old Testament saints will live in the New Jerusalem.

5. During the Eternal State, angels are needed to guard the gates of the New Jerusalem so sinful people cannot enter.

LESSON

		1	2	3	4	5	6	7	8	9	10	11	12
QUESTION	1	F	T	T	F	T	F	T	T	F	T	F	F
	2	T	T	F	T	F	T	F	F	T	F	T	F
	3	T	F	T	T	T	F	T	T	F	T	F	T
	4	F	F	F	F	T	T	T	T	T	F	F	T
	5	F	T	F	T	F	F	T	F	T	T	T	F